Business Life of Husband & Wife

Ins And Outs And All The 'Bouts

Clint & Robyn Pigeon

FriesenPress

One Printers Way
Altona, MB R0G0B0
Canada

www.friesenpress.com

Copyright © 2021 Clint & Robyn Pigeon
First Edition — 2021

The following information is intended as a general reference tool for understanding underlying concepts and practical applications of the subject matter covered. The opinions and ideas expressed herein are solely those of the Authors. Strategies outlined in this book may not be suitable for every individual and are not guaranteed to produce results.

Characters in this book for certain chapters have been fictionalized for educational content.

All rights reserved.

No part of this publication may be reproduced in any form, or by any means, electronic or mechanical, including photocopying, recording, or any information browsing, storage, or retrieval system, without permission in writing from FriesenPress.

ISBN
978-1-03-911195-0 (Hardcover)
978-1-03-911194-3 (Paperback)
978-1-03-911196-7 (eBook)

Business & Economics, Entrepreneurship

Distributed to the trade by The Ingram Book Company

TABLE OF CONTENTS

INTRODUCTION ix
    What Are the Three Greatest Challenges? xi

CHAPTER ONE: TWO MINDS ARE BETTER THAN ONE .. 1
    Myth 1: Men and Women Are from Two Different Planets 2
    Myth 2: Inevitability of Divorce 6
    Myth 3: Not Accepting Help and Doing Everything Yourself Will Work 8
    Myth 4: Sacrificing Your Career or Relationship 9
    Takeaways From Chapter 1 15

CHAPTER TWO: BEING BPLPS WITHOUT THE BS 17
    The Pros 18
    The Cons 22
    Keys to Being BPLP (Business Partners and Life Partners) 25
    Takeaways From Chapter 2 29

CHAPTER THREE: THE SWOT ANALYSIS..........................31
    Takeaways From Chapter 3..41
CHAPTER FOUR: AGREEING TO DISAGREE......................... 43
    Stuff We Agree About... 44
    Stuff We Disagree About (that We Can Remember). 48
    Where Do We Find Common Ground?........................52
    Takeaways From Chapter 4..53
CHAPTER FIVE: THE CANOE TEST 55
    Story Time 58
    Takeaways From Chapter 5... 67
CHAPTER SIX: THE TRAILER TEST AND THE NAVIGATION CONUNDRUM... 69
    Part I The Navigation Conundrum 70
    Part II The Trailer Test 74
    Takeaways From Chapter 6... 76
CHAPTER SEVEN: THE WIFE'S POINT OF VIEW 79
    Takeaways From Chapter 7... 87
CHAPTER EIGHT: THE HUSBAND'S POINT OF VIEW....... 89
    Takeaways From Chapter 8...94
CHAPTER NINE: SEPARATING HOME FROM WORK 95
    Takeaways From Chapter 9... 101

CHAPTER TEN: THE LIFESTYLE ADJUSTMENT 103
    Morning (Part I): 103
    Morning (Part II): 104
    Afternoon: 105
    Evening: 105
    Repeat 106
    Takeaways From Chapter 10 109

CHAPTER ELEVEN: BURNOUT 111
    Simple Signs You Are Burning Out: 113
    Takeaways From Chapter 11 117

CHAPTER TWELVE: WHY WE CONTINUE TO DO IT 119
    Sociology 120
    Psychology 121
    External And Internal Factors 123

CONCLUSION (IN HINDSIGHT) 127
    Our Five Core Principles of Communication 128

APPENDIX 131

BIBLIOGRAPHY 135

This book is dedicated to:

All the hardworking people who dare to take the ultimate risk of starting a business with their spouse, life partner, or other half.

And thank you to all the wonderful people in our lives who have allowed us to be able to write this book. You know who you are!

INTRODUCTION

Congratulations! You have opened a book that will either terrify you or motivate you (or maybe a little bit of both). The crazy-ass idea of not only starting a company but running one with your spouse can be a daunting task. Trust us. We've been there, and we're still alive to talk about it.

Our goal is that as you read each chapter of the book, you will be inspired to do something truly great with your partner while at the same time gain a better understanding of the trials and tribulations you may face moving forward. You may be in for a bumpy ride, but it is completely worth it.

Business Life of a Husband and Wife is our take on how to successfully begin and then scale up a business with your significant other as your professional partner. We want to show you what we have done and learned during the past seven years while running our company,

Two Birds Furniture Inc. This book is a candid look into the inner workings of our relationship as we navigate the world of business while trying not to start a fight in a grocery store parking lot because one of us forgot to grab milk.

Before going further, we want to let you know what we are all about and how we got to the "let's write a book" point in our journey.

Both of us (Robyn and Clint) grew up in Southern Alberta, but we didn't meet until 2012, at a roulette table in Las Vegas, Nevada—no joke. Robyn was in Sin City for a wedding as the maid of honour, and Clint was a young man, fresh out of firefighting school in Laredo, Texas, making a pit stop before heading back to Alberta. We took a gamble or two in the casino that weekend, and the rest is history. Two years later, we made a couple of small life changes, like getting married and starting Two Birds Furniture Inc. together (do you catch the meaning of the name now?).

Both of us had business experience prior to meeting one another. Robyn operated an equine physiotherapy business for twelve years, and Clint had had two minor companies during his time at the University of Lethbridge. Let's just say, we both knew we were unemployable by anyone except ourselves!

Two Birds Furniture started in a ten-by-ten basement room in the undeveloped area of a condo we were renting. It was a treat and a pain in the ass all at the same time. It was like having a delicious bowl of ice cream and suffering from brain freeze. Nevertheless, if you fast forward six years, we are now running a successful business, making some money, and living our life the way we want it.

So, what happened in those six years that got us to where we are today? This is why you need to read the book because the Coles Notes version will only get you a C– (and Clint would know because it's how he passed university). But first, let's look at the challenges of starting a business.

What Are the Three Greatest Challenges?

The biggest problem we have found during the past seven years is that most people in the world have a fear of failure. That fear is predicated by external factors that play on our emotions and render us useless in confronting that fear and overcoming it. In owning a business with your life partner, that fear could be the fear of becoming another statistic in the ever-increasing divorce rate or the fear of what family or friends will think if bankruptcy looms or the fear of how the outside world will look at us if we completely botch this opportunity and don't become successful and/or make a complete ass of ourselves. But, really, who cares? Life is about experiences, trials and tribulations, failures, successes, and just trying things you've never done before!

The second-biggest problem is the stigma around romantic working relationships. We've found that once you take the plunge as a couple and start a business, investors look at you like a time bomb waiting to blow. Furthermore, friends and family think you won't be successful because they couldn't ever imagine working all day with their spouse and then coming home and sleeping with them. However, some of the most successful people in the world are couples: Tom and Giselle, Jay-Z and Beyoncé, Barack and Michelle Obama. They are household names that have made it big together.

The last obstacle (and the most important) is the possibility of complete and utter communication breakdown. This is when things go nuclear, which is why it is the entire premise of our book. When starting a business relationship with your romantic partner, it's very easy to forget to leave your baggage of the day at the office or at home. The bleeding of boundaries is common in our society. Having work emails on personal cell phones and Zoom calls at the same table where you eat dinner are just a couple of examples of overlap. We may not be perfect at engaging in dialogue, but we have found a pretty good way to separate out the emotions when discussing topics of conflict with one another.

We are going to showcase our fears and how we overcame some of the challenges addressed above, and how we dealt with others to get through the good, the bad, and the ugly of running a company together. We are not going to deliver a solid-gold strategy for success, or some dumbass playbook for you to follow step-by-step. Rather, we want to show you what happens when you take on the biggest relationship stress test there is—managing money and emotions. Lastly, we are going to dive into our common-sense approach to communicating with one another and explain how we separate our home life from our business life while being able to integrate them both into our lives.

All our tests, perspectives, and personal experiences will tie into to our **five core principles of communication**, which are:

1. Trust
2. Honesty
3. Acceptance
4. Balance
5. Sixth sense

Each one of these will be explained in detail as you take the journey with us.

So, buckle up. Enjoy the book. Take a few things away from it to incorporate into your life and the journey you are on with your spouse, partner, or other half. Oh, and try not to kill each other while you're doing it! Embrace the unknown, the fear, the failure, the success, the bouts, and the ins and outs.

CHAPTER ONE

Two MINDS Are Better than One

One of the most important things you need to do before starting a business is recognize the myths floating around out there. We're not talking about the gods and heroes of Ancient Greece and Rome, but rather the illusions that many people have about the business world. We all know that every great idea starts in the mind, but so do really bad ones. In 2000, Blockbuster had a chance to buy Netflix for around $50 million, but the VHS rental giant wasn't interested. One went belly-up, and the other is now a multi-billion-dollar enterprise. It's inside our heads where choices are made, thoughts are given life, and plans of action are created. This is why we will explore and debunk **four** different myths about going into business with your partner/spouse in this chapter by using the acronym MINDS. And yes, we know there are five letters in that word.

The Myths:

1. **M**en and women are from two different planets
2. **I**nevitability of divorce
3. **N**ot accepting help and
4. **D**oing everything yourself will work
5. **S**acrificing your career or relationship

Myth 1: Men and Women Are from Two Different Planets

Biologically speaking, men and women are filled with a cocktail of different chromosomes and hormones. You may have even heard the famous saying that men and women are from different planets in our galaxy. John Gray wrote an entire book about it. At times, it feels like the differences between men and women have been analyzed to death in order to make money off of people's insecurities. And while some days it may feel like we are living on different planets, we are all human at the end of the day. Even though our sex may be determined at birth, our actions and choices are what ultimately define who we are, regardless of how we go to the bathroom.

Our choice to enter into a business venture together was not one we took lightly. We had people tell us things like, "Your brains aren't wired the same, and therefore, you won't be able to make it work long term." Even though one of us wore a dress to our wedding and the other wore a suit, our ultimate goal for our marriage, just like for our business, was the same. Our two minds needed to work as one if we wanted to be successful. But let me tell you, it wasn't all sunshine and rainbows.

At the beginning of most relationships, we have stars in our eyes and lofty fantasies about the future. If you've ever been in love, you know the beginning is like a golden sunrise. It's beautiful, but it's also blinding. Everything is going so well and then POW! Life hits you right in the kisser. Problems bubble to the surface and the differences between you are really put into focus. Disagreements and fights between partners in a relationship are common. You both start throwing the yellow penalty flags on the field, but there is no referee to blow the whistle. Arguments and discord are the basis for essentially all the plot development in any romantic movie or novel. *The Notebook* just wouldn't be the same without a little drama between Allie and Noah. However, the key factor is how each person comes out of that disagreement and shifts his or her mindset moving forward into the next discussion.

It's important to note that in our society there are forces and pressures at play that want us to believe that men's and women's brains are more different than they are the same, but that simply isn't true. Over time, these incorrect assumptions have become societal norms, which many have accepted as fact. Men love sports. Women love shopping. Men love power tools and hunting. Women love makeup and days at the spa. There are countless advertisements and commercials that play on these stereotypes. However, one of the most significant of these incorrect assumptions might be that men are logical and women are emotional.

The myth that men lack emotional intelligence and don't express their feelings is something that needs to be dispelled. Men can be emotional. If you've ever been in a room with a bunch of guys during the Stanley Cup playoffs and their favourite team is playing, you know what we mean. There is yelling and sometimes even tears. Alternatively, women can certainly be logical. Neil Armstrong and the crew of Apollo 11 probably wouldn't have made it to the moon without the contributions of female programmers and scientists working for NASA at the time. They needed the minds of both men and women to make the mission a success.

Even though we aren't rocket scientists, we have both had to work at overcoming our own biases to understand each other better for the good of our relationship and our business. It's easy to make assumptions about the way each of us communicate, which might be why divorce rates have skyrocketed in the last few decades. This is not just a one-dimensional issue, either. Jealousy, insecurities, and past experiences all contribute to the way we react to certain situations. It can be a vicious cycle sometimes, but the downward spiral can be stopped. If we can realize that the vast majority of our fights with each other are due to our own egos and inabilities to look at multiple perspectives, progress can be made. Also, when we come to an agreement that both of us have unique strengths and weaknesses, we are able to utilize those strengths and weaknesses for the common good. This notion will be discussed in greater detail in further chapters.

Ultimately, understanding your partner is about open and honest communication on all topics. Going into business with your spouse carries with it considerable risk, and if there isn't a foundation of trust, it's only a matter of time before the building will crumble. Trust and speaking the truth are absolutely critical. Secrets cast unwanted shadows, and those dark spots in a relationship can eventually become a cancer, which leads us to the second myth.

Myth 2: Inevitability of Divorce

Odds are pretty good that you know a couple personally or you know of one that has been through a divorce. According to Statistics Canada, the divorce rate for couples that were married in 1955 was 0.27 per 1,000 marriages, but by 2001 that number had jumped to 26.08![1] That's nearly a one hundredfold increase in fewer than fifty years. The reasons for the staggering increase in divorce rates can be attributed to numerous factors. However, one of the root causes may be that so many people are searching for greener grass on the other side of the fence instead of attempting to fix what's broken. The throwaway mentality has become a societal norm, and we have reached a point in society where the consequences for our actions have less permanence. Each year, humans toss millions of items into the garbage that could otherwise be fixed. Cell phone doesn't work? Throw it away and buy a new one. Small rip in your jeans? Most likely that pair is going to be dumped or donated instead of mended. But what happens when a relationship reaches a breaking point? It all comes down to choices.

We all make choices on a regular basis. Some are as simple as selecting what to eat for breakfast, while others

---

1 https://www150.statcan.gc.ca/t1/tbl1/en/tv.action?pid=3910002801. Accessed Aug. 2020.

are more serious, such as buying a Ford or a Chevy. Choosing a partner is also a choice. In any relationship, but especially one in which romance and business intertwine, the consequences of those choices are amplified for a number of reasons. For example, unlike spouses who have jobs at different places, going into business with your partner means sharing an office at work and a bed at home (unless somebody has been demoted to the couch). Furthermore, stress at work about projects and deadlines and clients can creep into the household. However, we've learned a few tricks to keep our relationship (and business) strong despite the storms. Divorce doesn't have to be the end result just because there are pressures we experience simultaneously.

One of the most important lessons we've discovered during our journey is that it's essential to check your ego. You have talents and skills that give you confidence as an entrepreneur, but so does your partner. Will your partner's abilities and decision-making prowess affect your level of success? Absolutely. If you're in business together, you need to be able to create synergy. In other words, your whole needs to be greater than the sum of its parts. When you can achieve that, it will not only make your business stronger, but your relationship as well. Divorce becomes a foreign word from a distant land, but that doesn't mean you won't have the occasional situation to work through.

You're an entrepreneur, so problem-solving is part of the job description.

Being an entrepreneur also gives you much more freedom and independence than other jobs, but that doesn't mean that you're always right. In fact, admitting when you need a helping hand can be one of the most liberating feelings, especially if you ask the right person for it.

Myth 3: Not Accepting Help and Doing Everything Yourself Will Work

In the workshop at Two Birds Furniture, there are occasionally large projects that require more than one of us to accomplish without injury. Lifting barn doors, assembling tables, or installing wood mantels can be done as solo projects, but they are much easier with more than one person. Similarly, you can run a business by yourself. Many do it, but eventually the tasks become more than one person can juggle and all the balls come crashing down.

It's been said that to be successful you need help, and there's a reason for that! Even the most successful and wealthiest people in the world needed a push in the right direction. Billionaires Oprah Winfrey and Richard Branson both had support from their partners to get where they are today. Not one of us is truly a one-person show. Some like to think that they are, but behind the scenes, there are almost always some amazing partners, spouses, or employees who help them shine. Asking for help doesn't mean that you're weak. It means you're strong enough to know how to navigate through a tough situation. We also all need a stable environment in which to thrive, and that starts with who is in your corner. And who better than your spouse?

Myth 4: Sacrificing Your Career or Relationship

Do you like ice cream? Even if you don't, let's assume you do. Do you like pie? Again, let's say you do. Can you eat each one of those foods on their own? Why, yes, you can. But, can you also enjoy each one more by putting them together? Indeed.

Ice cream is like your career and pie is your relationship. Or maybe it's the other way around. Regardless, you don't need to sacrifice one for the other. It's possible for them to mix, and many couples actually combine these very effectively. On the other hand, some are like oil and water, but that's not what this book is about; better leave that for your shrink with the PhD to help you with.

You've probably also heard the term "work-life balance." Rather than thinking about your life at or away from work as a scale that needs to reach equilibrium, consider the metaphor of a light switch instead. You either love the game or you don't. You love what you're doing or you hate it. You either jump in and take a chance or you don't because you're scared of risk. There is no dipping your toe into the pool from the high diving board.

Your personal definition of success is up to you and your partner to discuss. It's important to set those boundaries in order to create a fulfilling life for both of you. When Two Birds Furniture was still in its early stages, we both had our own insecurities, and often there were more questions than answers. But eventually, we got to a point of comfort with our situation and the life we wanted to lead. You don't need to pick between your career or your relationship. Good news. You can have both and be happy!

It was the spring or summer of 2012 when we started going on dates more regularly and establishing our relationship. Almost all couples at the beginning of a relationship want to see each other as much as possible, which is natural, and helps to develop deeper feelings. This wasn't the case for us at all.

Clint was erecting buildings in a variety of rural locations, and Robyn was on the show jumping circuit with her business. Both ventures resulted in long days, weeks, and months. As a result, this left minimal time for one another, and worse yet, the only time we had for one another was between jobs. This meant that when we did see each other, we were often either irritable, exhausted, and feeling less romantic than the average Joe. We had a choice to make and work to put in if we wanted our relationship to take root and start growing. We had to learn how to communicate more effectively.

When it comes down to it, life is about choices, plain and simple. Coffee or tea? Skirt or dress? Fries or salad? We make a decision and then we move to the next, and so on and so on. Each decision leads to another, and some are definitely more complex and lasting than others. One of those important decisions is picking a lifestyle and a partner that aligns with your vision of success, even though sometimes it's not blatantly obvious at the time. Two Birds Furniture is evidence of the choices we made. We decided one day to commit to starting a business together. Rather than complaining during our growing pains and blaming each other for the crazy things that happened along the way, which can cause resentment, we wanted to air out our dirty laundry and put it in a book, undies and socks and all!

So many people in the world today like to complain about things and come up with reasons as to why things won't work/shouldn't work. Here are some of our favourite excuses we've heard about not being able to work with your spouse:

- ❖ **We have to have family time.**

    We all need that for a healthy life, but it's how and when you choose those moments that's important. It's not necessarily being home every night for dinner at five o'clock to make your spouse happy. You can be creative with family time by bringing the kids to the office when possible. Is it the fact that you're all home at a certain time and sitting around a specific table that makes it a family dinner? No, that fact that you are together makes it a family dinner! Make them part of your team and give them safe and meaningful tasks to do. At the end of the day, it's your business.

- ❖ **I don't have time.**

    Yes, you do. Each of us is gifted twenty-four hours in a day, and we make choices about how we spend it. This one is the worst excuse in the history of excuses. We both firmly believe that you make time for what you find important. If you love exercising or find joy in reading, you'll find time to do those activities. Therefore, the excuse of not having enough time is a weak one. Too many people use this as a crutch to avoid starting something, such as a business, with their spouse or something else they are passionate about. In short, try something new. Take a risk. What is the absolute worst that can happen?

- **I'd kill him/her if we had to work together.**

    This is a popular one with the most serious of consequences. Here's a free tip to avoid spending time in criminal court and/or a correctional institute: First work on your relationship, sort out some of your issues, and read this book. We've been in this game for almost a decade now and neither of us have come that close to jail time, except for that one time that . . . better leave that part out.

- **I like to have space.**

    Yes, so do we and pretty much every person we know. Find your space and communicate your needs to your spouse. It's easier to explain it to him or her rather than hiding out in a nine-to-five job that you don't even like. This is all about honesty.

    Here are a few options to consider for creating space and time for yourself:

    - ◇ Book a hotel room for a night or two for yourself every few months.

- ◇ Take yourself to a bookstore and explore the shelves (maybe even buy this book for a friend or family member).
- ◇ Go out to a coffee shop with your friends without your other half.
- ◇ Find a hobby you love doing—hockey, scotch tastings, dress club, horse clinics, and going to the gym are few we use.

❖ **We wouldn't last long term.**

This excuse is like giving up on a race before you even start. Think back to the third myth (not accepting help and doing everything yourself will work). You can get better together if you shift your mindset from INdependence to INTERdependence.

Rather than experiencing an *implosion*, your relationship and business can experience an *explosion* of energy, renewal, and innovation if you put the time and effort into it. If both of you are willing to make your relationship and business work, be confident that it will.

The key is seeing the bigger picture rather than focusing on the short-term bumps in the road. If you've ever driven on a gravel country road, you know that it isn't always a smooth ride. There are a few stains in our truck due to spilled coffee because of just that. However, if you let a pothole or two demoralize your entire trip, well damn. It happens and then it's done. The rest of the journey and the destination is the real goal, not just a couple rough spots.

Clint's great-grandma Grace Colemen used to say, "Oh poor you," anytime someone whined about anything. She was one tough woman who lived through the Great Depression and World War II. The majority of our generation has no reference for the real hardship of those periods. In general, we have it relatively easy compared to our ancestors, and we still recite many of the same narratives as they did seventy to eighty years ago.

Takeaways From Chapter 1

- ❖ Dispel the myths around working with your spouse (the MINDS acronym).
- ❖ Remember, two minds are better than one.

CHAPTER TWO

BEING BPLPs WITHOUT THE BS

Some things in life just can't happen at the same time. You can't turn left and right at the same time, and you can't land a coin heads and tails simultaneously. A face card in a deck can't be diamonds and clubs. Fortunately for us, we believe...check that, we *know* that it's possible to fulfill two roles at once. Spouse. Business partner. We're living proof that it can be done.

In this chapter, we are going to discuss why we chose to work with one another over having separate business partners to start our company. But fair warning, it's not a choice to be taken lightly. Before we agreed to diving into an enterprise together, we had to weigh the pros and cons. Because we've already taken that leap of faith, we thought we'd save you the time and show you how we reached that decision.

One of the most brilliant minds in American history was Benjamin Franklin. This is the guy who is responsible for giving the world bifocal glasses and the lightning rod, as well as having his mug shot on the United States one-hundred-dollar bill. In addition to inventing practical items and having his face plastered on piles of money, he also devised a way to make tough decisions by weighing both sides of an argument. This method of making difficult choices also saves time and provides clarity to the decision maker.

Here's our list outlining the pros and cons of having your spouse as your business partner:

The Pros

Focus 24/7—Working Toward the Same Goal

Why is a laser more powerful than a single lightbulb? The answer is simple. It comes down to focusing energy toward a single point. When you're physically with the same person around the clock, you have time to invest emotionally with each other. Once you make the effort to invest intellectually as well, it's possible to start developing and attacking the same goals together. When two minds are focused on the same objective, the odds of achieving it increase significantly.

Familiarity/Consistency— Better the Devil You Know

This old adage is a reminder that sometimes it's better to be with the one you know than the one you don't. In business, this is particularly important for a number of reasons. First, if your spouse messes up, you can have a discussion about it over dinner or on the drive home or during *The Bachelor*. Secondly, you know how each other tick. It's much easier to fix a broken watch if you know what all the pieces do. Similarly, if you know how your spouse operates, you'll have a better chance of repairing anything that's broken. Sometimes our watches are a little out of sync, but with the right tools, they can be adjusted. Lastly, it comes down to communication. You and your spouse should have open channels with each other so that you can voice any problems or concerns, or at least, we hope so. Usually couples have this natural way of talking with each other, and that's one of the reasons why you're together, right?

Trust—Relationship Is Already There

Any engineer or construction worker will tell you that building a house or a high-rise building requires a solid foundation. If you lack one, that structure probably isn't going to last for very long. When it comes to relationships between individuals or groups, trust is that foundation. Usually relationships need time to develop that trust, which is normal and reasonable. What's abnormal and unreasonable is thinking that you can enter into a relationship or business with others without first establishing that trust.

With a spouse, you know you will always have someone in your corner of a fight, and trust us, there will be fights of many different varieties. There will be conflicts that arise with staff, clients, suppliers, and landlords, just to name a few. The business world is full of friction and competition, and you'll need a solid corner mate to go into a war room with you.

Building and Bonding—
Growing Together

When you're starting and running a business, it's almost inevitable that you will experience change. You'll learn new things, make mistakes, and take risks. All of these will allow you to mature as a person and a business owner. Therefore, it's only logical that you do that growing together and reach new heights as a team rather than individuals.

Any time that you start a new adventure, there's a very good chance you'll be uncomfortable at some point. Travelling to a new country where they speak a language you don't know or starting a new school are both scenarios where people often experience unease. But getting out of your comfort zone is where so much growth happens, and when you work with your spouse, you already have a built-in support system to make the unknown just a little less scary.

Reaching the point of exhaustion can make or break some people. But if you want to be successful, you need to push through when you're tired. Working with your spouse affords you the luxury of built-in empathy. Right by your side is someone who is experiencing the same trials and tribulations as you and understands the grind.

Moments of anger and frustration will arise at some point during your business journey. When either of us is pissed off about something, we have a sounding board. The pressure valve can be released, so to speak. This doesn't mean that your problems will go away, but rather, they occupy less space in your brain because you've had a chance to vent. The money you'll save on a shrink can go toward a new couch for your house, instead of paying to go lie down and talk in an office somewhere else.

Feeling pretty inspired? I would hope so, after all those points listed above. Who wouldn't want all those things running like a well-oiled machine? But every coin has two sides, and our list is only halfway complete. Benjamin Franklin didn't shy away from the other side of the argument, and neither will we. We've shown you the good, but here's the bad and the ugly of working with your spouse.

THE CONS

BLURRED LINES—CONFLICT FROM WORK CAN FIND ITS WAY HOME

For most people, a crappy day at work can be salvaged by a relaxing evening with their family in the evening. However, one of the risks that comes with working alongside your spouse is the carryover effect. Butting heads at work like a couple of fully grown elk can continue in the kitchen (with minimal damage to glasses and plates, we hope). Yet, arguments about who washes more clothes or who leaves dishes in the sink can happen to people who work two different nine-to-five jobs as well. In the grand scheme of things, it's all pretty small stuff, though.

Familiarity/Consistency—How Much of the Devil Can You Put Up With?

This one should look familiar. Yes, familiarity/consistency is on the pro list, but there are days where the devil is just a little more evil than usual, if you know what we mean. Sometimes the devil is on a rampage, and you'd best get out of the way. It's always helpful to practise ducking for cover because it can feel like a hurricane full of piss and vinegar.

Mixed Emotions—Romance to Resentment

Relationships are dynamic. They are full of ups and downs. They ebb and flow. They are raw, and sometimes, emotions can get the best of you in a situation. It's normal to feel resentment when something you don't like or expect happens. But what's more important is how you choose to react to what happens. Feeling is part of being human, and what we've found is that it's important to let your feelings be known, whatever they may be. When disagreements fester over time, they have the potential to become more volatile and explosive.

Mixing marriage and business just adds another layer of complexity to both. That doesn't mean you should let emotions hold you back from being a better, stronger, and more resilient couple as a result of conflict. In fact, you need those rough patches to test your mental fortitude and earn a few badges of WTF happened along the way. Currently, we're working on the "I made it through an argument without swearing" pin for our sashes. Ultimately, practising self-control and educating yourself and your partner on each of your triggers is the key to ensuring there's more romance than resentment in your relationship.

Separation—Parting Ways

Fighter pilots have an eject button for getting themselves out of a tight situation; couples have separation or divorce. This is the ultimate risk of entering into business with your spouse. However, there are plenty of people who aren't in business together that drift apart and file for divorce. Plumbers get divorced from bus drivers. Lawyers get divorced from police officers. It happens across multiple occupations. But if this possibility is what's holding you back, don't let it drive your relationship or your businesses. Put that fear in the backseat, or better yet, throw it out the window (and into the closest garbage bin, of course). Rather than hitting eject, try the reset button instead.

People fight and straws break the backs of camels, but reconciliation is always possible if you're willing to check your own ego and enter into that process. That being said, there are still some things that fall into the no-fly zone category. Cheating is one them for us. It would be over in an instant if one of us decided to forget our marriage vows and our commitment to each other. We made those for a reason, and at the end of the day, we are in this together. In addition to those lines we spoke to each other on our wedding day, we've also developed some strategies, or keys, that have helped us unlock the secrets of being both a business partner and a spouse (BPS) and avoid the BS. This isn't some CIA level spy stuff, and it's worked for us.

Keys to Being BPLP
(Business Partners and Life Partners)

As we mentioned earlier, there are five essential elements of effective communication. There needs to be trust, honesty, acceptance, balance, and a sixth sense. As you look through our list of keys to being a successful spouse and business partner, you'll see these principles woven within.

Constant Check-ins

These allow us to discover where we both are emotionally and mentally, and have quickly become a way for us to charge forward. We have to be honest with each other. The check-ins are simple yet so effective in that they allow us to take each other's temperature, so to speak. It can be as basic as saying, "How are you really doing?" Being aware of our own emotional and mental states has spared us from getting into (some) unnecessary arguments and conflicts. We still have the occasional dust-up, but those can also be quelled by using a touch of humour and playfulness if the situation warrants it. Check-ins not only allow us to get a sense of what the other person may need, but they also keep our minds sharp. We're able to have a better understanding of each other because it opens up channels of communication and allows us to have a sense of how things are going within a given moment, day, or week. Consistency also allows us to develop that **sixth sense** we mentioned before because we get better at reading and understanding each other.

Goal Discussions

Talking about our short-term or long-term objectives involves **trust** in each other. The conversations can be as simple as a quick discussion in the truck on the way to work or a full staff meeting in the shop, depending on how large or complex they are. We also have a system in place, though, that allows us to compartmentalize our goals. For example, if it's a personal goal, like buying a property in Hawaii or the Teenage Mutant Ninja Turtles arcade game that you never had as a kid but have dreamed of owning for over twenty years, we keep the discussion at home or outside of work. Recently, one of these personal goals was achieved, much to the chagrin of one of us (Turtle Power!). But, if it's a professional goal, like hitting certain sales targets, we find a time slot with one another and put it on the books. There also needs to be **acceptance** with our shared goals for them to be worth pursuing.

Team Meetings

Your business or organization really starts to gain momentum as you add more staff. Companies like Apple, Microsoft, and Amazon, which had only a small handful of people in their beginnings, have ballooned into enormous enterprises, with employees in the hundreds of thousands. It's a pretty safe bet to assume that even large businesses like the big three mentioned above still have staff meetings to discuss important issues. The ones we have at Two Birds Furniture may not take place in a twenty-fourth-floor conference room with a mahogany table and leather chairs, but team meetings are crucial for the health of any organization. They help achieve that important **balance** that every successful business needs. As mentioned previously, we each entered into our intimate and business relationship with a unique set of skills, strengths, and issues we needed to work on sorting out. As we added team members to our staff, we recognized the importance of ensuring we had opportunities for each individual to voice concerns and ensure we were all on the same page because sometimes it seemed like we weren't even reading the same book! Team meetings help clarify expectations and create an environment of continuous feedback. They allow us to be **honest** with each other.

ARGUMENT ANALYSIS

The last key is one that we use when (and not if) we have an argument. They can range from a little tiff to moderate spats to full-on nuclear meltdowns in the most extreme cases. How do those arguments end? Was the issue resolved? Were we both satisfied because we were heard and the other understood our perspective? Or was one of us the hammer and the other the nail, so to speak? Reflecting on the different outcomes of our arguments can give us an idea of our state of mind at the time and what may need to work on in order to continue successfully. Argument analysis is just one of the ways to find **acceptance**. It's also important to be a spouse or business partner that your counterpoint will want to be around.

Using techniques and various methods to analyze other aspects of your relationship should be another crucial step in your journey. Why do some couples from *The Bachelorette* make it, while others don't? Why has Larry King been married eight times, yet Denzel Washington and his wife, Pauletta, have stayed together since tying the knot in 1983? Those are other mysteries that we won't even attempt to answer. But what we do know is that it is absolutely essential to have an understanding of the dynamics between you and your significant other, as well as your comfort level for working so closely together. You want to be more like Han Solo and Chewbacca and less like Walter White and Jesse Pinkman. That's why the next chapter is dedicated to a relationship SWOT analysis. What on earth is that? Well, keep reading to find out.

Takeaways From Chapter 2

❖ Open communication is the goal; ongoing dialogues verbal and nonverbal about your goals, strategies, and thoughts are incredibly important to building a strong foundation.

- ❖ Honest and consistent communication is the key; positive or negative, it is important to your relationship's overall growth.

CHAPTER THREE

THE SWOT ANALYSIS

When you hear SWOT, do images of heavily armed law enforcement units come to mind? If so, you may be thinking about SWAT (special weapons and tactics). Rather than knocking down doors and rappelling from roofs, in this chapter, we'll be focusing on how a SWOT analysis can help provide you with insight into yourself and your partner, as well as serve as a framework for building and structuring your business.

So...what exactly is SWOT?

In short, SWOT is a tool used to identify an individual's, group's, or organization's **s**trengths, **w**eaknesses, **o**pportunities, and **t**hreats. It can also be broken down into two components, which are internal and external factors. The SW (strengths and weaknesses) fall into the former, whereas the OT (opportunities and threats) belong to the latter.

Think of it like this: You have control over what you're good at and what you need to improve. Person A might be phenomenal at fixing cars, but can't write a speech. Person B might be one of the greatest orators of a generation, captivating millions with his or her words, but doesn't know the difference between an alternator and a piston.

On the other hand, there are just some things that are out of your control. These are the external factors. For example, not too many people could have estimated the impact of the COVID-19 pandemic. In addition, who knew barnwood doors would have become so popular in the last decade? Some of these are threats, and others are opportunities. It's important to differentiate between them, but to learn from each, which leads us to the next question.

Why complete this task?

By categorizing your ideas into these four distinct categories, you are bringing organization and clarity to your business and to yourself. The SWOT analysis can (and really should) be done before you start a business, as well as during your journey. You might be asking yourself,

"Why is this so important?" The answer lies in the Five Ws (who, what, where, when, and why).

This tool can illuminate the deep and complex relationships between individuals and **why** people act a particular way. You need to understand this in order to determine **what** the tougher tasks will entail when running a business. Furthermore, this tool makes it apparent **who** can and cannot manage different aspects of the day-to-day, and **where** skills can best be utilized. It also brings clarity in terms of **who** needs to take the lead on certain tasks and **when** it's appropriate to do so. Lastly, the SWOT helps to explain **why** roles within the business are what they are. There's a reason why one of us takes on the day-to-day planning and execution (Robyn), and the other plans for five to fifteen weeks down the road (Clint). If we were to visit an optometrist, the doctor might say that one of us is nearsighted and the other is farsighted. We may both need a strong prescription for glasses if we were on our own, but together, our vision is 20/20. Having a clear view of the future, whether it's near or far, is also essential in an ever-changing economy.

The business word is not static, which is why it's crucial to revisit the SWOT periodically in order to re-evaluate those internal and external factors because they can shift. Markets and business plans can also change, which is why the SWOT should be a living document that's updated regularly. Hopefully, over time, your weaknesses transform into strengths and threats become opportunities for growth. Ultimately, it should "lead to fact-based analysis, fresh perspectives and new ideas,"[2] which, if used correctly, will only help your business flourish.

Here, we'll give you a look at our business dynamics and show you what our own SWOT analysis looks like. There are two empty templates in the appendix that you can fill out for yourself.

---

2 https://www.investopedia.com/terms/s/swot.asp. Accessed Aug. 2020.

Partner #1 – Robyn's SWOT Analysis

Strengths

- Focus/structure
- Work ethic
- Putting goals into action
- Learning ability
- Day-to-day execution

Weaknesses

- Long-term planning
- Fluid communication
- Thinking I don't need help
- Sensitive/emotional

Opportunities

- Willingness to learn
- Persistent
- Likes people
- Ego

Threats

- Never think I am prepared
- Take on too much
- Burnout
- Listening to others

Partner #2 – Clint's SWOT Analysis

Strengths
- Creativity
- Work ethic
- Passion for the process
- Diverse skill set

Weaknesses
- ADHD – completing projects
- Temper – run hot
- Thinking I don't need help
- Enjoyment of people

Opportunities
- New business opportunities
- Always looking for more
- Willingness to try
- Drive to succeed

Threats
- Lack of empathy
- Ego
- Always looking for more
- burnout

We don't want to bore you with a lengthy and deep analysis of our own relationship, so here is a very quick recap of each of our SWOT charts. When you complete this for yourself, we encourage you to explore it in further detail with your other half. But remember, the weaknesses shouldn't be used as ammo later on or a wish list of things you want the other person to fix. Here's a breakdown of our SWOT.

STRENGTHS — Our strengths are ideal for a start-up because our combination includes a planner and a go-getter while also having a double dose of strong work ethic. One has the ability to constantly generate new and innovative ideas, and the other has an adaptive learning capacity to execute those ideas. One of us lines them up and the other knocks them down. Apple Inc. wouldn't be the company it is today without the dynamic pairing of the Steves. Steve Jobs and Steve Wozniak had complementary skill sets that translated to success. Wozniak played the hands-on role of the engineer, while Jobs came up with the brilliant ideas. Although Jobs was more in the spotlight, together they changed the world.[3]

WEAKNESSES — This is an area where we start sharing some similar traits, which can bring out both of our

---

3   https://www.entrepreneur.com/slideshow/297885#9. Accessed Sept. 2020.

emotional sides (extra sensitivity in Robyn and a temper in Clint). We are both very aware of what happens when we transform Dr. Jekyll to Mr. Hyde, which is why we use daily check-ins. If we don't make time to touch base with each other, we know it'll be like walking through an emotional minefield. Acknowledgement of your weaknesses is the lock; knowing when to refocus on your strengths is the key. It's incredibly important to be open and honest with your spouse in this discussion and be accepting of each other's downfalls so you can lift each other up.

OPPORTUNITIES — Acknowledging your collective strengths and weaknesses creates and magnifies opportunities to grow within your relationship. Reflecting on them makes it possible to combine your mind with your partner's. Remember, two minds are better than one! For instance, both our SWOT charts reveal that we both have a willingness to try or learn new things. This opportunity is both a strength and a weakness for us, but it affords us the chance to use each other's strengths so we don't fall flat on our faces. A prime example of this happened a few years ago.

Story Time! "How It Went Down" (according to Robyn)

I was sitting at the front desk with a cup of coffee when Clint came into the showroom one morning with an idea. Sometimes I treat his ideas like a farm cat by giving them a little pet and then leaving them alone for days. But this one was different.

After he had gotten the team started, he decided now was the time to add more products and details to our showroom space. It was definitely on our list of things to do eventually, but there were about a thousand other tasks we also needed to get done in the meantime. Not to mention, we had already planned more than one new addition to the showroom, so it could wait. Doors needed to be built, tables needed stain, and I really wanted to check off some orders, but Clint...well, he had other plans.

It's important to note that Clint has a tendency to start multiple jobs at once. If he wasn't in the furniture business, there would be a career for him in the circus as a juggler. So, when he started putting up new wainscoting, I knew we were in for a treat. He got about three-quarters of the way through before his squirrel of a brain decided to move along to the next project, which involved hanging doors. But before the doors were hung, a new banquet was being built. Now, he always manages to complete the projects (even if it nearly kills him), but the process drives my very linear brain batty. It's usually up to me to use my strengths and help guide the situation along so that Clint can finish the tasks he's started. Moments like this allow me to turn Clint's weaknesses into a strength for our relationship.

THREATS—We don't want to actively focus on the threats too much because there will always be outside forces that are looking to derail your plans. Whether it's friends, family, clients, or competitors, we don't feel that focusing attention on the outside threats or voices are worth the time or energy. It's important to acknowledge them, but you should never let them dictate your decisions. Awareness of threats to your lifestyle choices, business goals, opportunities, and relationship are vital to your success, but not if they hinder your abilities to execute your goals.

You are going to need more than just the SWOT analysis to work on the nuances of your relationship. We've already come to terms with the fact that figuring that out will be a lifelong process. But at least it's a launch point. Completing this task will allow you to better understand yourself and your partner so you can help each other and grow as a couple and be better business partners. The SWOT task is not for everyone. Call your therapist if your relationship worsens or you have significant and drastic changes in your behaviour! Mild side effects may include headaches, insomnia, increased appetite, and mood swings, but also increased productivity, a healthier relationship, and a better understanding of your partner. As authors, we take no responsibility for the path on which this may lead you.

When you get a chance, fill out the SWOT analysis. There's one for you and one for your spouse or partner. Use this tool to learn about each other and become comfortable with the uncomfortable. Over time, and if you engage in constructive conversations, you will grow as a couple and realize if you're compatible to start a business with one another. It's not for everyone, but when it is, it's magic.

Takeaways From Chapter 3

- ❖ The SWOT analysis is a business tool that can be relevant to evaluating your future compatibility to work together with your spouse.
- ❖ Honesty and acceptance are two of our five core communication principles.

CHAPTER FOUR

Agreeing to Disagree

Part of any healthy marriage or relationship is the ability to find common ground. Each one of us is unique and full of our own thoughts, ideas, and feelings about how the world should and shouldn't be. When two autonomous individuals decide to enter into one relationship, there will be times when ideas clash, but there's a reason why a single battery cell has two ends. It requires both a positive and a negative terminal in order to function properly and for electricity to flow through it. Much like a battery, sometimes we are diametrically opposed to each other's ideas, but that's what makes our relationship work. Our differences in opinion, taste, and other preferences aren't always that far apart though. We do have some fundamentals that we agree on, but also a list of others we don't. And somewhere, amongst all of that, we still find common ground too, proving that we're a little more sophisticated than batteries after all.

Stuff We Agree About

One of the most important points that we agree upon is our long-term and financial goals. We have a common vision about where we want to be as a couple, as well as a business, in the next five to ten years and beyond. Furthermore, we share the same financial targets for ourselves and our business. In our personal lives, even though one of us would prefer buying dresses and the other arcade video games, our overall objectives are the same. We have regular discussions about our finances and the goals we would like to reach for our business. Sometimes we hit them and sometimes we don't. What's important is that we have a common understanding and an idea about where we would like to be in the future. Speaking of the future, another thing we agree on is our vision statement.

When we started Two Bird Furniture, it was important for us to generate a vision statement. Say you are inviting your friends or family to go on a road trip with you, the vision you present would essentially tell "your traveling companions where you are going . . . [and] if anyone wants to go on that journey and arrive at that destination, they should consider getting on board."[4] If they don't like where the journey is headed, they don't need to come. Developing a vision statement for our business established which direction we were headed and gave us a destination to try to reach. Our vision statement is:

To create, design, and build dreams out of history.

At Two Birds Furniture, we use reclaimed wood to build our products, so each piece has a unique story to tell. Old barns, bridges, sheds, and other buildings that have been vacant for years or decades are given new life when we turn them into furniture for our customers' homes. Our goal is to take their vision, make it a reality, and offer them a piece of history they can enjoy for years to come.

Customer service is another key area that we agree on as a couple. It really is the fuel that ignites and sustains any business. Gaining the trust of clients and establishing a relationship is one thing, but maintaining that connection is another. Our goal with customer service is to be quick when responding to any concerns, as well as being clear and concise when communicating with potential or return clients. Like any business, we've had our fair share of challenging customers, but we've learned from those

---

4 https://www.inc.com/peter-gasca/understanding-vision-mission-in-a-simple-analogy.html. Accessed Aug. 2020.

moments and grown stronger as a business and business partners. Without customer service, your business will erode and eventually become spoken of in past tense. Even though both of us are actively involved with customers, there are other parts of the business that require distinct roles.

Just like the human body, the designation of roles in any business or any organization is necessary for the survival of the whole. Hands and fingers don't look the same as feet and toes because they serve different purposes. Similarly, there's a reason why roles like CEO, CFO, COO, and VP exist in the corporate world, and why Wayne Gretzky or Mario Lemieux didn't wear goalie equipment in the NHL. Gretzky and Lemieux were two of the best at making sure pucks went into the net and not keeping them out, leave that part to Patrick Roy or Ken Dryden. Whether it's professional hockey or business, giving individuals specific roles allows them to focus their energy on that one component and ensure it thrives. At Two Birds, we have a clear separation of duties. We stay in our lanes so that we don't go off the rails. Why is staying in your lane important? Staying in your lane allows the business to benefit from your strengths, your partner's, strengths and your team's strengths.

Lanes aren't limited; it just means you focus on what you're good at. Drive your own cars, but stay on the same road. Continue to increase the lanes with your partner's support as you enhance your knowledge base, increase your efficiency, and execute your goals. Also, build a team that complements your core values and enjoys the drive you're on.

Let's compare our business to a work of art for a moment. Clint is able to identify trends within an artistic movement. He is able to determine the layout of a new creation, as well as which elements would work best together. But Clint is not much of an expert with a paintbrush in his hand. That's where Robyn comes in. She makes sure each step is executed according to plan, and every brushstroke is done with precision and care. In the end, both artists are essential to the completion of the piece, but each role is distinct.

Ultimately, it comes down to the trust we have in one another. In order for our business to be successful, we need to have faith that the other person is going to do their job, and is going to do it well. Otherwise, we would end up with something resembling a finger painting done by a toddler instead of a Picasso. But just like in art, not everyone has the same taste, and there are some areas where we disagree.

Clint & Robyn Pigeon

Stuff We Disagree About (That We Can Remember)

The beginning of episode twenty-six from the fifth season of *The Office* shows a proud Kevin Malone walking into work with a large pot of his famous chili. The recipe has been passed down through generations. In addition to toasting his own ancho chiles, he was up the night before "pressing garlic and dicing whole tomatoes." He even lets the audience in on his trick of undercooking the onions to ensure everybody gets to know each other in the pot. Unfortunately for Kevin, his chili also gets very familiar with his suit and the carpet in the office, but that's not the point.

Chili is one of those foods that allows for latitude and has plenty of room for creativity. Those who are serious about chili will argue whether or not beans belong or if turkey can be used as a protein. What about the level of spice? Should a spoonful light your mouth on fire or just give you a subtle hello? Much like the interpretation of what a proper chili should be, we also have our own feelings about some things. If we were to continue with the chili analogy, here are three categories where our views do not align:

◈ The recipe (the steps to get to our end goals)

- Cooking time (hours of work)
- Heat vs. sweet (finding balance between our work and personal lives)

The Recipe

There are people that like to get from point A to point B as quickly and directly as possible. That's Robyn. Then there are those that tend to wander around. They might take the backroads, shortcuts, and the occasional drive through a farmer's field. That's Clint.

So, which one do you agree with? Are you more like Clint or more like Robyn? We still have common long-term goals, but we just happen to disagree about the best path to reach them. Does this create tension? We'd be lying if we said it didn't. In the end, we both know that we're going to end up with a delicious pot of chili, no matter the recipe. But that also leads to the next area of disagreement. How much time do we want to commit to this pot of food?

Cooking Time

If you've ever made a great soup, stew, or chili, you know it takes time. Let's pretend it's 1995 and the Instant Pot isn't around yet. Like Kevin Malone said, the ingredients need time to get to know each other. But how much time is enough? And is it possible for them to get to know each other too well?

Here's an argument from each of our vantage points:

Clint:

If I had a job in the circus, it would definitely be a juggler. Three balls is for amateurs. Four is even a bit too easy as well. Most of the time, I have five to six tasks going on at any given time, which requires time. For me, eighty to a hundred hours a week is the sweet spot to hit weekly targets. More hours equals more work. More work equals more money. Simple mathematics.

Robyn:

If Clint is the juggler, I would definitely be the ringmaster. Although I completely understand his basic arithmetic, Clint sometimes forgets that more work also equals less time at home. For me, sixty hours is a reasonable ceiling. Within that time frame, I can lay out what needs to be accomplished and be as efficient as possible. There's some truth to the "work smarter, not harder" slogan. During the weekend, I like to be able to shut off my work brain and recharge.

Again, who do you agree with more? Are you more of a marathon or a middle-distance runner?

HEAT VS. SWEET

An exceptional chili has layers of complexity and multiple flavours happening simultaneously. In the end, it should be a symphony of onions, garlic, tomatoes, meat, and spices. But how much spice are we talking about? Fire breathing dragon level or "Hey, I feel you"? Much like our taste in how spicy or sweet a chili should be, finding an equilibrium between work life and personal life is another area where we don't see eye to eye.

Clint:

There is no such thing as a balance between work and personal life. Both are intertwined and it just comes down to priorities.

Robyn:

There IS such a thing as balance. Clint believes there isn't. I believe there is. Case. In. Point. Each of us needs time to rest and refocus. There is a world beyond work, and burnout happens when that realm isn't explored enough.

Despite all these areas of disagreement, we do actually get along quite well most of the time. Why? Well, we don't want to end up like Kevin Malone and his poor pot of chili. Being able to make compromises and work through our differences is one of the main reasons why we're still together and haven't completely abandoned our business and filed for divorce. So, in what areas do our minds actually meet?

Where Do We Find Common Ground?

The answer to the question above is quite simple. We find common ground by utilizing our weaknesses to maximize our strengths. How is this achieved? Another short answer—the SWOT analysis. This tool allows us to focus on the long game rather than get caught up in day-to-day bickering. By analyzing ourselves and our traits, we are able to leverage our skill sets and align our goals and targets. It's all about finding that sweet spot.

Millenia ago, the famous Greek philosopher Aristotle argued that maintaining the Golden Mean is the source of all virtue in life. In other words, "in order to find happiness, people should always strive for a balance between two extremes."[5] This is why finding common ground, or the Golden Mean, may be the answer to finding the perfect balance and partner to execute on your business goals!

Takeaways From Chapter 4

- ❖ It's okay to have your own preferences and to not agree about everything.
- ❖ Play to your partner's strengths—stay in your lane.
- ❖ Communicate to find common ground.

---

5   https://medium.com/@perezanthony/why-aristotle-was-right-the-power-of-balance-b743f82edc9f. Accessed Oct. 2020.

CHAPTER FIVE

THE CANOE TEST

The canoe test is simple yet extremely informative. It can't be done in a classroom or with pencil and paper. If you made it through high school by copying off your smart friends, this is not one of those exams. Rather, it requires a couple to get outdoors and into nature. After that, the steps are actually quite easy. Give two individuals each their own paddle. Put said individuals in a boat on open water. Then, sit back and enjoy the show.

We have a theory about relationships, and one way to test our hypothesis is with the canoe test. This simulation has resulted in some pretty funny and unexpected stories, which we will share later in the chapter. Based on our experience with this test, we've discovered that each iteration results in different outcomes because no two couples are the same. After researching this topic, we've found numerous articles, journals, and studies related to the test that all highlight the power of a canoe, two paddles, and open water. Beth Dreyer explains the canoe test by stating that it "can bring to light how [couples] handle unexpected challenges together...exacerbate a power struggle... and induce a blame game."[6] The experience of paddling a canoe together as a team reveals so much about a couple. It allows you to see your partner's strengths and weaknesses within a self-contained water vessel, free from the distractions of the modern world.

It's also important to note that there is some scientific evidence to support our hypothesis. One study found that couples who engage in demanding physical activities together have a deeper level of intimacy and enhanced relationship quality.[7] As a bonus, we have some great memories of canoeing together ourselves, as well as watching the chaos unfold with other couples, and sometimes even with ourselves. And each time we paddle with other couples and witness the test in action, we experience the Baader–Meinhof phenomenon. The what?

---

6   https://www.rd.com/article/canoe-relationship-test/. Accessed Oct. 2020.

7   Aron, A., Norman, C. C., Aron, E. N., McKenna, C., & Heyman, R. E. (2000). Couples' shared participation in novel and arousing activities and experienced relationship quality. *Journal of Personality and Social Psychology*, 78, 273–284.

Also known as frequency illusion, the Baader–Meinhof phenomenon (*pronounced "bah-der-myn-hof"*) is a cognitive bias. That means it happens in your mind and affects your judgment. The Baader–Meinhof phenomenon happens when you're exposed to something new (dog, person, clothing) and then suddenly you start noticing it popping up everywhere. After browsing for a new vehicle, have you ever started seeing the ones you've been looking at everywhere on the road? Or have you ever noticed how many athletes use filler words and sounds like "um," "er," and "you know" when getting interviewed by the media? Not to spoil your enjoyment of TV shows set in Southern California, but if you ever watch one (*e.g., Keeping Up With the Kardashians*), take a drink every time a person says "like." Chances are you'll be passed out on the floor before making it through an entire episode. That's frequency bias in action.

So, because we're aware of the theory behind the test, when we take couples out on the water, we are subject to the Baader-Meinhof phenomenon. Either way, the experiences we've had make for great stories to share and have allowed us to understand our own idiosyncratic behaviours. But enough talking about the test, let's see what has happened to couples on the water who have been brave enough to try the canoe test.

Story Time

As you read each mini-story about the canoe test, we invite you to identify threats and opportunities from the situation. Consider and discuss with your partner what can be learned from each experience. Remember, this book is about whether or not you can (or should) partner with your spouse to run a business. Think about which strengths can be used as the foundation for starting a business together and the weaknesses that might cause an unravelling if not dealt with, and whether they can be turned into strengths.

One last important note: The couples mentioned in these stories don't work together and names have been changed to protect their privacy.

Story 1: Lake Paddlers

Steve and Carly had never gone paddling in a canoe before, and in the first few minutes together, their lack of experience was quite obvious. In addition to their lack of nautical knowledge, they also decided to spice things up by bringing their dog along for the ride. Maybe they thought he could provide some direction and order, but alas, this was not the case. Unfortunately for them, their dog was as clueless about paddling a canoe as they were. The lack of arms and fingers also meant he couldn't even lend a hand if things went south. Check that. When things went south.

Once we had helped successfully launch the canoe for Steve, Carly, and their dog, the issues began. The troubled trio just couldn't manage to travel in a straight line. Instead, they settled into an S-curve pattern for the entire length of the pristine lake. From our vantage point, rather than gracefully gliding along the water, their technique looked more like a cat scrambling to get to the shore. And just a few minutes into their journey, frustrations boiled over and the verbal assault began. If Steve and Carly could paddle as well as they could swear at each other, they would have potential to be Olympic champions.

The constant swerving of the canoe, along with the cussing, was too much for their canine friend. He couldn't stand it anymore and jumped out of the canoe in one smooth motion. We couldn't trust Steve and Carly to make a ninety-degree turn, so we rescued the dog and began to paddle back to shore. After spelling out more letters in the water with their paddles, our friends made it back to shore eventually. Once they reunited and apologized to their dog, they informed us that sharing a canoe wasn't really for them and they probably wouldn't be getting into a boat together again for a long, long time. Upon hearing those words, their dog gave a wide, beaming smile and began wagging his tail.

It can be argued that canoeing requires a specific skill set and only improves with practice. It's true that once a pair of individuals get into a rhythm, it's not all that complicated. However, the old adage of being easier said than done definitely applies to this situation. Steve and Carly quickly discovered that talking about how to paddle and canoe straight and actually doing it while on the water are two different things.

The goal of the canoe test is to learn to work with, rather than against, one another. It's about achieving harmony instead of discord. Solving problems and making adjustments on the fly while in a canoe is important because when you get into the daily operations of running a business, you will have multiple tasks going on at once and decisions to make with large implications. Furthermore, there are almost always new distractions that will require problem solving as a team and pivoting on the fly to survive.

So how does all of this relate to part of the SWOT analysis from Chapter Three?

- ❖ **Threats:** Distractions, poor communication, lack of skill and technique.
- ❖ **Opportunities:** Inexperience—the couple can use this adventure to start a new hobby, knowing what they need to work on, and break down the tasks.

Story 2: River Rafters

Unlike the previous couple, the day started out great for Dave and Dennis. There were laughs, smiles, and a general feeling of merriment all the way to our first destination. Things were easy, but maybe that's because we were travelling with the current. Much like an old river, the situation for Dave and Dennis took a sharp turn sideways on our way home. It could have been fatigue. It could have been hunger. It could have been a change in the planetary alignment. Whatever it was, their paddling became sporadic, choppy, and out of sync. The couple soon fell far behind our group, and then things went from bad to worse. Once Dave and Dennis were alone and way behind the pack, the seeds of disagreement that were sown earlier began to sprout.

Their asynchronous paddling soon led to even more discord. Sharp words and even sharper glances were exchanged between the once happy couple. What was happening firsthand was that one person was over paddling and overcompensating because of their anxiety of being behind the pack, while the other member was blissfully on holidays and not in a hurry to catch up—hilarious to watch from afar but not so funny for the couple in the boat. They eventually both just stopped in the middle of the river! Making things worse, we were all paddling against the current figuratively and literally on a river, and therefore, they were now going backwards. Now at this moment, the couple realized they were both at fault for not being in the situation they both wanted to be. Although one was on holiday and the other was stress paddling, they both, at the end of the day, wanted to keep up with the group. They did eventually catch up, and we laughed at their comical responses to each other while they were in earshot.

We are not trying to make light of the misfortunes of others, but most of the time having a fight on solid land is much easier than having one on the water in the same vessel in tight quarters. Nevertheless, this canoe test can provide some valuable lessons. When discord happens in a microenvironment, it is a sign of potential problems when faced with a larger issue in a macroenvironment, and that is the major point of the whole canoe test theory.

As we all know, it's very tough to get anywhere in this world without some sort of help or guidance. It's even more difficult if you have a partner that is on a different wavelength than the other when you need him or her the most. The basic goal of canoeing is to steer your ship *together* in a forward direction to reach a given destination. This may sound simple, but when only one person is doing one hundred per cent of the work, or over compensating while the other is not paying attention or communicating, it can potentially shift your individual strengths into weaknesses as you try to juggle too many tasks. In addition to paddling straight, imagine trying to add five or six more tasks to that list. Answering a phone. Taking a photo of the picturesque scenery. Turning left at a certain point in the lake. Finding and eating a snack to refuel. Diffusing an argument with your partner who has different goal in mind. Oh, and it's your first time paddling a canoe and now there's a snake in the water! It's tiring just thinking about how to manage that scenario. Inevitably, it becomes too much and you end up making a mistake (or multiple mistakes). Running a business alone can be like this. It is an upstream battle, and you need help. It's as simple as that.

Let's pull out one threat and one opportunity from this experience.

- **Threat:** Ego. In short, a lack of empathy and awareness for others in the moment. This, along with a strong sense of individualism can cause communication to break down.

   Note: Everyone showcases these traits at certain times, and it's about the acceptance of your flaws and communicating that with your partner.

- **Opportunity:** Communication skills. This couple has identified this as an area for growth and can now work on turning it into a strength.

Story 3: Ocean Kayakers

Until this point, we've shared two stories of the canoe test playing out on the relatively calm water of a lake and a slow, meandering river. However, switch the vessel to a kayak and the setting to the ocean, and things get more interesting and even a little dangerous.

Canada borders three different oceans, so there are plenty of spots to find adventure and trouble. Unlike freshwater lakes, there are riptides, currents, sea life, and other complexities to contend with. Nevertheless, a couple we know on the East Coast decided to take a trip out on the water one beautiful day. Or was it just a fair day? Regardless, the trip started out with golden rays of sun dancing on the water. Our fearless couple was thoroughly enjoying their ocean escapade. However, their reverie had made them blissfully unaware of how many coves they had paddled past, and they were unsure of exactly where they were. In addition to the navigational conundrum they found themselves in, our happy paddlers also noticed that the sun had disappeared behind some dark clouds and the sky had turned from blue to dark grey. We're no weather experts, but generally you want to be on land during stormy weather if the only thing between you and hundreds of feet of water is the plastic shell of a kayak. And so the fearless couple did what any normal pair of people would do in that situation: they started to let their emotions take over.

Now, emotional responses are a natural reaction to uncomfortable situations. They can be perceived as positive or negative, depending on how you respond to them. Both individuals, Ken and Deb, realized their situation, and even during a heated debate on rhythm and urgency, they began to communicate their thoughts and feelings. In order to find the inlet, they had to paddle back out into the ocean to locate a familiar landmark on shore. This allowed them to paddle their way into a more manageable situation. The major issue they faced was making it to shore in a timely manner as efficiently as possible, without getting lost and caught up in the looming storm. Because neither of them are Olympic athletes, it was going to be a task! The risk of going back out into the ocean posed its own challenges, but allowed the couple to gain a different vantage point and defuse the situation. The most important part of this story is that they made it to an inlet safely and they were able to dodge the incoming weather.

The basic goal of any task is to be able to complete it safely and effectively (or before danger arises). This story emphasizes the point that two individuals can benefit from having different strengths and weaknesses. This couple exhibited similar weaknesses, which ultimately got them into a dangerous situation. It also showcases that when put into a stressful situation beyond your control, weaknesses can develop into strengths. Put into perspective, both parties may have become emotional but were not irrational and were able to adapt quickly together to safely get to shore. Had they both become irrational, this story could have led to a very different outcome. Developing these skills of adaptation on a micro level is the most important thing you can do as a couple, so when you are working together in a macroenvironment with multiple moving parts, you can both work together to adapt and solve the big problems.

- **Threats:** Blissfully unaware, the couple has the same set of weaknesses.

   Note: Unexpected circumstances beyond your control can arise at any time.
- **Opportunities:** Adaptability; the couple was able to turn weaknesses into strengths.

Takeaways From Chapter 5

- Personality types and traits within people or yourself are going to have a direct impact on the dynamics of relationships.
- You can't change your natural disposition or what you were born with, but you can adapt.

- ❖ Small sample sizes and scenarios are much more revealing about a person's character, especially when an individual is under stress or in an unfamiliar situation. This becomes amplified when situations become more complex.
- ❖ Partner or support systems are important for successful relationships.

CHAPTER SIX

THE TRAILER TEST AND THE NAVIGATION CONUNDRUM

Another test? Why, yes, of course. If you've been around the business world long enough, you'll know that you're constantly being assessed and evaluated. Week by week. Day by day. Hour by hour. So why not apply some important principles of business to see how they play out in other facets of life? Just like starting your own business, this test is one that reveals character and is more about that sixth sense you develop with your partner. This chapter is broken down into two parts and it's all about recognizing how stress influences and impacts behaviour and communication. The canoe test was about moving forward together, but the second part of this chapter is about going backward to achieve your goal. But before we get to the test, let's take a look at what happens when you're attempting to figure out the way to your goal.

Part I
The Navigation Conundrum

Even though we've moved beyond relying on printed out instructions from MapQuest to find unfamiliar addresses, one fixture has remained in the vehicles of countless couples around the globe. We're not talking about rearview mirrors or cupholders. This component even predates air conditioning and power windows. You may be so familiar with it that you might shudder at the next few words. It is, of course, the backseat driver.

Picture this. A leisurely Sunday drive with your spouse. No pressure, just a casual cruise on the open road. All of that would be possible if it were not for the backseat driver. "The light turned green." "Watch out for that guy." "Slow down." "Speed up." These are just some of the phrases that might be uttered from a backseat driver. And then there's the nonverbal actions. The grasping of the handles in panic. The rolling of the eyes. The crossing of the arms. All of a sudden, this relaxing Sunday drive has turned into a highway to hell. After being berated for what you've been doing behind the wheel, you're now ultra-aware of all your decisions. You're driving with the same confidence as a fourteen-year-old kid with a newly minted learner's license. And how do you, a shaken conductor, respond in this situation? Put simply, it goes back to our basic human instincts. Fight, flight, or freeze. Since you are strapped in by a seatbelt and there is nowhere to flee, often verbal punches will be thrown or there is awkward silence and the occasional gasp.

Now imagine this. Instead of the leisurely Sunday drive, we are now transported to a crowded, busy, unfamiliar city where the population drives on the left side of the road. It's rush hour and car horns are playing their daily symphony. Instead of traffic lights, intersections are governed by traffic circles. Left turns are now safer than right turns. Asking for directions is useless because you can only understand about one third of what's being said. Top that off with narrow roads covered in puddles from the constant rain, and welcome to Edinburgh, Scotland.

This is the navigation conundrum, and it's all about anticipation. If you've ever been behind the wheel in a new city and your navigator (spouse) is running the GPS, you know exactly what we're talking about. A veteran shotgun passenger is always a few moves ahead of the driver on the map. Frustrations can reach a boiling point if directions aren't given at the right time or incorrect turns are taken. It's all part of the fun, and it gets even more interesting if there are a pair of Type A personalities involved. If this is the case, the inside of your vehicle may look like the Fourth of July with all the fireworks going off. Or maybe, just maybe, you show off your incredible teamwork and reach all of your destinations unfazed and unscathed. You won't know the answer until you've been in that situation.

Our Navigation Conundrum Story

Before flying across the pond to Scotland, Clint had major reservations about driving around in the downtown core of any city. For the first ten years of his driving life (age sixteen to twenty-six), he avoided congested areas similar to this like COVID-19. After all, Clint grew up on the open range and was more familiar passing tractors on the highway than with one-way streets. Robyn, on the other hand, was an All-Pro city driver.

Because she had travelled around the country for several years with her first business, she was no stranger to the busy streets of the inner city. Unconventional traffic patterns and navigating avenues with more than two lanes was a breeze for her. Therefore, when it was Clint's turn to drive in Edinburgh, Robyn knew she would have to become the sensei and he the pupil. The power of anticipation.

Throughout the trip, Robyn helped Clint get past his anxieties when driving in major city centres by being clear and concise when traffic was heavy. This allowed Clint to stay more relaxed when maneuvering through high traffic volume and get to each destination safely. Over time, Clint has learned to stay more levelheaded and calmer when a turn is missed. Instead of flying off the handle or swearing like a sailor, he has become more adaptable to unexpected situations.

If you pay close enough attention to your spouse's behaviour, these types of situations will reveal the type of person you will be dealing with when you decide to run your business venture together. It takes time. It takes practise. But the more you work at it, the better you will be able to anticipate problems, and the better you will become as a team. It's also important to remember your strengths and weaknesses. Remember the SWOT analysis? What can you work on to be a more productive team member, and are you willing to work in this? Just like riding in a car, you will need to rely on each other to reach your goals in one piece and on time. Nobody likes to wait on the token late couple at a dinner party, but sometimes navigation conundrums do happen.

Part II
The Trailer Test

If the navigation conundrum was about anticipation or your sixth sense, the trailer test is centred around the communication of your sixth sense (as is the majority of this book). This test involves understanding each other's body language, hand signals, and curse words when backing up a trailer. Oh the joys of trailers. When you turn left, the trailer goes right. When you go forward, the trailer should also go forward if you attached it properly. Take a turn too sharply and you may take out a signpost. It's all part of the adventure. Whether you're a weekend-warrior couple who love to take the RV camping, or a business owner hauling products to tradeshows and making deliveries, your basic driver's licence handbook has about seven pages on this topic. What they don't tell you in the book is how to navigate backing up a trailer with your trusty sidekick in your rearview mirror yelling directions.

And this is how battles proceed in the usual manner, and probably why the rearview camera was invented. You turn left, they point left and you turn right . . . into that lovely poplar tree that was going to create the perfect shade cover for your weekend getaway. A busted taillight and a bent bumper later, the pullout is now malfunctioning and it's nine rounds or nothing between you two.

Unfortunately, the trailer goes the opposite direction of which the driver turns the vehicle, and this is one of those minor communication details that can spark dissent among the ranks.

Moving backward, aka backing up a trailer, in its simplest form, is about communicating left and right—when left and right are opposite. The problem there is that every person has a different way of communicating or a different set of signals.

Story Time

So, now the trailer is parked, and everyone is enjoying the fact that the trailer is in its final resting position. Joe is looking for an axe and is out of vocal range from Martha, who has decided to cool down by the river. He yells, asking for the location, and cannot hear her response. In frustration, Martha chooses hand signals to help. She pats her front, followed by two taps to the butt. Joe, in utter confusion, throws his hands in the air and draws a question mark in the sky. After a few minutes of using the same signals, with no results, Martha walks back to the trailer and within earshot states, "It's in the box behind the seat!"

Learning your spouse's/partner's mannerisms and problem-solving style can you put you ahead in situations similar to and larger than this simple test. Predicting their moves, opinions, and input comes with time and further develops with the connection that you have; however, sometimes your partner changes those signals halfway through the task (Clint) and you have to start all over again! We digress, yet, developing your and your partner's ability to pick up on these cues on a smaller scale is hugely valuable when you begin moving ahead into potential bank meetings, pitches to investors, and day-to-day client interactions.

You will have developed the understanding of reading your other half's nonverbal way of communicating even if you don't realize it. It's your sixth sense!

Takeaways From Chapter 6

- ❖ Nonverbal communication is learned over time and through a series of unfortunate events, which become important events to recognize.
- ❖ Discovering your partners nonverbal stress responses in certain situations and learning how to respond to those situations allows for effective results.

- Plan ahead and anticipate changes; everything is always moving backwards and forwards, and adaptive communication is a huge value-added learned response for the future success of your relationship goals.

CHAPTER SEVEN

THE WIFE'S POINT OF VIEW

We'll take the next two chapters to dive into our two different perspectives, personalities, approaches, idiosyncrasies, and emotional states. In this chapter, I (Robyn) will talk about what I do to ensure our business and partnership is successful.

I thought a good place to start would be explaining my background and where I came from before starting Two Birds Furniture. I have been happily unemployable my entire adult life, and before the joint venture with Clint, running a business on my own was simple and straightforward. I could do things my way, when I wanted, and on my own terms. My daily routine was predictable and comfortable. I had a simple business model that was broken down into a few simple parts.

I was involved in the high-end service industry of equine physiotherapy. My patients were horses, but my clients were their owners. However, I had limited contact with the latter and spent most of my time driving to different appointments, performing treatment, and doing administrative work. Simple. Straightforward. I repeated this formula for more than fifteen years of my life, but then everything changed after that night in Las Vegas when I met Clint. And by everything, I mean every single thing.

I, me, and mine turned into we, us, and ours. The hours I put into my equine business were now put into literally and metaphorically building a furniture company. Shifting from a simple, independent profession into a large, more complex one with my new husband was daunting. There were multiple new challenges I had never faced before.

Suddenly, there were more interactions, decisions that needed to be made quickly, staffing issues, deadlines, attracting investors, and adjusting to a new and unfamiliar industry. The learning curve was steep and unforgiving. Some days, it felt like trying to climb Mount Everest with a limited supply of oxygen and a seventy-five-pound pack. In a blizzard. Without a Sherpa. Wearing only a very thin pair of mittens. And the tent poles seemed to have disappeared. Okay, well maybe it wasn't that bad, but I can tell you with one hundred per cent certainty that I was stressed to the max.

My body started to feel the effects of this, and the stress manifested itself in very peculiar but obvious ways. After about nine months into building our new business, my body started to send big, glaring warning signs to slow down. In my nightly shower, I would reflect on the day, think about the next one, and then stress vomit. This never happened to me when I had my own business, so why was it starting now? I was a seasoned vet with over fifteen years of experience owning a company. Ah, but those were the simple, straightforward, comfortable times. This new undertaking was none of that. After consecutive days of the shower vomits, I was struck with the harsh realization that I needed to do better at finding a balance with my mental, physical, and emotional health. Unlike before, this time I didn't need to go through this alone. I had the best partner by my side to help me find equilibrium again—my husband.

I can tell you wholeheartedly that there are countless differences between a solo business experience and a partnered business experience. There are benefits to both, but there are more upsides to working with a teammate day in, day out. Time and experience (the two great teachers) have revealed this to me. I've come to value collaboration more than independence. Having someone with whom to bounce ideas around, exchange stories, and discuss the future is truly irreplaceable, but that doesn't mean it's easy. And if you knew my husband like I do, my patience is really put to the test some days. There are days when I wish we were in a canoe so I could paddle his stubborn ass into the lake. But there's also nobody else I'd rather be in business with.

As a solo entrepreneur, I often felt lonely and isolated. Nobody could really understand what I was going through. No one could relate. Ultimately, it felt like I was spinning so fast on a merry-go-round that I couldn't get off and land safely back on the ground. Except I wasn't a seven-year-old child—I was a grown woman, but the ride was life and the stakes were much higher.

A trip to Vegas unlocked this door I never knew existed, and a new chapter of my life emerged. The idea of starting a business together was out of complete necessity. Remember, I was highly unemployable, and as it turns out, so was Clint. We were young but not naive. We were engaged but not yet married. We had giant dreams but limited funds. We had ideas but no real idea of how to execute them. We had the stereotypical building blocks of a start-up business. Oh, and our workshop space? A ten-by-ten-foot box of a basement in a city townhouse that we could barely afford.

The early stages of our business started out like most profit-orientated hobbies do. We asked friends and family if they had any interest in products that we were about to invest the next decade of our lives into. As you can probably guess, we had a mixture of responses. "I don't think that this is a good idea." "Are you sure you want to do this?" "Sure, of course, we'd be happy to check it out!" To be frank, we're both stubborn and didn't really put too much stock in all those voices. So, we dove headfirst into the deep end. Raising capital was one of our first priorities, and miraculously, we found some funding. Once that was secured, we began to look for a location. The ten-by-ten basement just wasn't cutting it anymore, and we needed plenty of room for all our big ideas.

We found a building. Check.

We discovered there were many expenses we weren't anticipating. Damn.

We were locked into a lease that was not ideal. Double damn.

We had a business plan. Well part of one. Half marks?

Oh, how funny a thing is hindsight. Looking back on those early days was like watching a toddler learn to walk. Our business experienced plenty of growing pains, but they were necessary for us to get to where we are now. The key for us was commitment and constant communication.

I work, live, and breathe with my forever partner. We are ultimately in it together. There were plenty of times when we both could have quit and walked away, but we stuck with it. And now, we know each other's strengths and weaknesses inside and out. Going through all of this together and being forced to work through issues has created the most solid foundation for our marriage. It's those difficult and challenging times that have strengthened us the most, but that doesn't mean they're in our rearview mirror. We're still learning about balance for both of us, and I often ask myself the following questions:

When do I need space? When does he need space?

When do I need support? When does he?

Am I communicating clearly what I need?

When do we both need to back off and catch up on sleep? (We've had so many silly arguments that neither of us remember the reason they started simply because we were both so tired.)

Learning the ebb and flow of this whole marriage thing isn't as simple as saying, "I do." It's complex. It's dynamic. And because we are both evolving as individuals, marriage itself has its ups and downs. We talk about everything. And I mean everything. Our achievements. The tasks we blundered. How we can improve things for next time. Then there's the silly mockery and bantering that breaks up the monotony and gets us through the day-to-day. I am also blessed with a kind-hearted soul of a husband, who also happens to be incredibly emotionally intelligent. He's aware of when I'm stressed and need to consider trying out one of my coping mechanisms.

For me, there are three keys to managing stress:

- My emotional support team
- My physical outlet
- Sleep

My emotional support team involves three different components rolled into one nice package for my brain. Firstly, I need animals. Why? Well, having animals around keeps the nurturing side of my personality happy and balanced. Tending to their daily needs helps keep me relaxed. I'm sure there's some psychological rationale behind this, but just trust me, it works. Secondly, I need time with friends. There's a core group of girls that have always been there for me. We ask each other questions, offer advice, and sometimes distract each other from life's problems. They also keep me sane and balanced, and I find they are my life's pause button. Lastly, I need family. Those unannounced appearances, calls, and flights across the ocean all bring me joy. And then there's my weekly Dad chats, Mum visits, and brother/sister and family evenings that are also important to me. My family helps keep me anchored and they provide consistency and connection. But, they are just one crucial element for managing my stress. I also need something that makes me sweat, which brings me to my physical outlets.

For over twenty-five years, I competitively rode horses. I was riding about five to six times a week, and it kept me happily distracted and fit for years. Unfortunately, I lost my last horse in 2016 and found it incredibly difficult to find another outlet. Due to recent world events, we had some time to upgrade our home gym, which now includes everything I will ever need in a home gym. Ultimately, having a physical outlet can help make those challenging days, moments, and clients just a little more manageable. It also allows me to be ready to tackle each day without baggage. Our motto has become these simple words of wisdom: *Leave your baggage at the door when you come in and take it with you when you leave.*

Lastly, the key to managing my stress is sleep. I have always been someone that requires a lot of sleep, and as a result I prioritize it. I need somewhere between nine to ten hours a night to keep my cognitive functioning at its best. Otherwise (and you can check with Clint), I can become a touch delayed, among other things. This was a valuable lesson that I learned early in our start-up phase, and I needed to make it known clearly. Communicating this to Clint was incredibly important because I needed to be at my best and he needed me to be at my best. This forced me to be honest with myself and trust that Clint would accept that this is something that I needed in order to maintain balance, not only within our relationship but in the office as well.

Looking back at my SWOT, you can see that fluid communication is something that I needed to work on, and am still working on today. That being said, I am focused on taking one of my weaknesses and transforming it into a strength.

Takeaways From Chapter 7

- ❖ Find out what you need to be your best and communicate it.
- ❖ Accept what your partner needs.
- ❖ Needing sleep is not a weakness.

CHAPTER EIGHT

THE HUSBAND'S POINT OF VIEW

In this chapter, I (Clint) will tell you a bit about myself and what I do to ensure our business and partnership is successful.

It's hard to pinpoint the exact moment when I knew that I wanted to run my own business. I can remember several occasions when I knew I couldn't work for anybody but myself. But, I did need to learn some hard lessons, and what better way to do that but by trial and error.

Solo business ventures are a totally different beast compared to ones with a partner or partners. There is no one with whom to bounce ideas around or empathize. No one but yourself to blame if things fail. Success depends on your own talents, abilities, and sheer willpower. My solo business venture was tough as hell, but it made me who I am today.

I started my first company and worked as a contractor doing various custom jobs for farmers and ranchers. I quickly found out that I couldn't keep up with the demand of customers, suppliers, employees, and behind-the-scenes tasks. I was only one human, which meant at some point during the day, I needed to attend to the most basic needs, like eating and sleeping. But those activities were distractions at the time. I could have been working twenty-four consecutive hours and still not be caught up, or even close. In the back of my mind, I knew that I needed help, but I was twenty years old with youthful energy and naivety. I thought I knew it all. Hell, some days I still think I do, but the school of hard knocks has an interesting way of cuffing you upside the head when you're out of line. Eventually, the long days caught up with me and I burned out, a topic we will discuss more in a later chapter. I figured that more hands-on-deck would ease some of the burdens I was facing. I needed to learn how to delegate tasks and share the workload. Yet, I had a tough time finding someone who was willing to make the same sacrifices as me and who had the same drive as me. In general, I find the majority of people are slow and lazy in comparison, so the search for a partner was not an easy one, but eventually, I did find a partner, not only in life but also in business.

I needed my partner to execute on my crazy big ideas and dreams and be willing to accompany me and accept me as I bounced through life. At the same time, I was out to prove a point that I was better than my partner. I could work longer hours, complete more projects, and generate more business. It was less like a partnership and more like an internal competition. I was young. I was immature. And I was emotionally unintelligent. Did I learn a lot of lessons? Absolutely. Was my first business a healthy business? Absolutely not. I could have continued pushing through, lining up jobs, and working long hours, but something was out of sync. I needed a change, or as they say in the business world, a pivot.

Let's start a business, we said! it will be fun, we said! Our first year in businesses was like trying to sail through a hurricane. The journey was not smooth. The sea was not calm. It was wave after wave of challenges with no clear horizon or end in sight. We had to juggle personal payments with rent and life. We maxed out credit cards, we bounced cheques, missed minimum payments, raided our parents' freezers, and just scraped by. But we never missed a company payment. Not once. We always found a way to make it work because we had to. It came down to making money or going hungry. We didn't have a choice.

We pushed. We leaned into the grind, and we didn't give up. Not on our business and not on each other.

At some point, our operation outgrew our basement and we needed a bigger space. With seed money from investors, we were able to buy our first real woodworking equipment and trailers for moving products, as well as open up our first storefront. Like most new businesses, we had growing pains. We took our licks from clients, ex-clients, shareholders, and critics, but we learned valuable lessons and got through it by doing a few simple things. One, we had many long hard discussions with each other about our strengths and weaknesses, work-life balance, and our ideologies about home and work; and two, we learned how we needed to communicate with one another, either verbally or nonverbally.

When Robyn and I started Two Birds, I realized the value of collaboration. I discovered a different side of myself. I needed to trust my partner and let go of certain things, tasks, and ideals that I had created during my first business venture. If you look at my SWOT in Chapter Three, one of my weaknesses is thinking I can do everything solo. By understanding my own weakness and allowing my partner to execute on her strengths, it helped us build a foundation for a better relationship and business. Also, looking at my threats and opportunities, I realized that I have the tendency to be a malcontent and that is shown in both sides of my chart. The reason its there is because I can make brash or rushed decisions on a whim sometimes, which makes it a threat to not only the business but the relationship.

For example: I had a Sunday afternoon off from all engagements, and without discussing with Robyn, I bought us a building in the middle of nowhere! I went to Robyn all excited and proclaimed, "We are proud owners of a hundred-year-old building in Empress, Alberta!" I looked for her to be excited as I was. She was not. She was shocked and then laughed at me because she was not surprised.

I have this tendency, and I know I do, and that is why I don't go to casinos without first setting a budget, as I can be impulsive and like the rush of the unknown... sometimes. This, however, is not what I am like when making decisions for the long term. I strategize, communicate, research, and analyse multiple scenarios, which makes it vital that I'm aware of my pitfalls in being discontent with the status quo in the short term. However, being a malcontent is also an opportunity, as it makes me constantly curious to keep pushing myself—and, let's be honest, keep Robyn on her toes.

Yes, we still have our ups and downs, but what couple doesn't? Over these past few years, I've realized that having a collective sense of unity, open communication about my impulsive side, and working toward a goal with my wife will be and has been more rewarding than any solo business venture because we have the same endgame in mind. Two minds are better than one.

Takeaways From Chapter 8

- ❖ You cannot do everything physically, mentally, and emotionally.
- ❖ Learn to diversify your tasks between you and your partner. Understand the threats and opportunities that come from your personality.
- ❖ A weakness is only a problem if you don't work on it, and threat is only bad if you don't acknowledge it and work at making it an opportunity.

CHAPTER NINE

SEPARATING HOME FROM WORK

When you think about it, we all wear different hats for different occasions. Some of us are uncles or aunts. Some of us are brothers or sisters. Husband. Wife. Manager. Nurse. Lawyer. Business partner. Colleague. But what happens when husband and wife are also working side by side on a daily basis? That's what this chapter is going to explore. The answer is simpler than you might think.

Knowing when it's time to work and when it's time to transition to home for the day is the key to being successful in your business and your relationship. Clint has a rule, which is as follows: "I am not your friend between nine a.m. and five p.m." After five p.m., if you have a personal issue, you deal with it then, but your staff and your clients come first between nine and five.

What this means is that there has to be a separation point during the day. For example, the construction worker who spends eight to ten hours on a jobsite isn't going to be wearing his hard hat at the dinner table that night. Similarly, a professional football player in the NFL doesn't take his daughters to dance recitals with his helmet on and chin strap done up. There are different hats for different occasions. Being able to separate the day's emotions and shut off that side of your personality from work mode to home mode is easier said than done.

The problems you may approach or experience as a couple are going to be different than those you experience as business partners. There has to be a clear divide between personal and professional relationships. Being angry at your spouse for something that has happened at home should stay there. At home. For example, a pet peeve of Robyn's is when Clint leaves the cupboard doors open, and he constantly hears about it. However, this minor grievance is only aired at home, and the annoyance Robyn expresses is shut off when we walk through the office doors. The old adage of leaving your baggage at the door applies even more so for couples that work together. It's important to change your mindset when maneuvering between work and home. Both worlds require a different side of you. You have to be able to flip into business mode and make decisions that have limited emotions attached to them, and then flip that switch in your brain to turn on the emotional intelligence side required for a relationship when at home.

This requires resetting your brain and adjusting your frame of mind and body language. You need to be prepared to approach problems and be ready to work on the business. Dealing with staff, clients, and anything else that arises throughout the day requires singular focus. With that being said, after the work day is over (*remember: you need to know when to work and when you don't*), you have to have a reset period in order to re-engage in husband and wife at home mode. The language you use and the emotions you show need to pivot back to your relationship and lifestyle goals. There are five key strategies we use to accomplish just that.

1. We **acknowledge** turbulent times. Rather than ignoring an issue, we let each other know that we want to dropkick the other person off a cliff. This happens in both work and home modes. You have to differentiate when you're angry about something personal versus something professional.

2. We **apologize** for our mistakes. Both of us have days when we realize lines have been crossed. When that happens, we have to set our egos

aside, say I'm sorry, regroup, reorient our mindsets, and remind ourselves what our endgame is!

3. We **utilize** our commute time to talk. We have a combined hour before and after work each day to discuss the business, new strategies, or any challenges we are experiencing or foresee happening. We also have our own decompression time once we get home. Although we try to eat dinner together whenever we can, we also set aside alone time for our own sanity.

4. We **work** when there's work. This means we're in the shop on weekends and most holidays. Usually, it's just for a few hours and is pre-scheduled (for Robyn's organized brain). Clint's ping-pong brain can do without set times.

5. We **learn** from the past instead of dwelling on it and make relevant changes. Our journey hasn't been perfect. There have been ups and downs. There have been arguments, and tears in the shower. But there also have been laughter and smiles. The key is taking lessons from each of those moments and moving forward to become a better version of yourself.

And that's all there really is to it. Keep work stuff in a work bubble and personal stuff in a different one. In other words, have a work version of yourself and a personal version of yourself. That doesn't mean you have to be fake, but rather professional. The way we chitchat with our friends certainly isn't the way we would talk to clients about serious projects. It's all about knowing when to wear our different hats because we're all capable of it. The key is knowing when it's the right time for each one.

Here are a few methods that we use, that are similar to most couples, to keep life simplified and separated. One, we have separate calendars: one strictly for business and everything that sits under that umbrella, and, another for all things personal, with each category having its own colour that is recognizable between us based on priority and importance. Example of this, we have all health and wellness bookings in red, all social engagements in blue, and holidays in yellow. Same for the business calendar—meetings are in teal, service is in red, and time away from the office is in black. Streamlining these details makes it easier to transition from business brain to home brain. Granted, there needs to be that window of decompression time allowed to each partner for that transition to happen. Two, we create spaces, certain spaces within both the home and office that function as a medium for us to transition from one brain to the next daily. What we have created, and might not work for everyone, are two spaces within our home that are used for decompression and recovery. One space is a full home gym, with a sauna to sweat out the tough days. The other space is our lounging area, where we can watch TV, work together on additional ventures (such as this book), and take naps. In the office, we have separate spaces in different areas of the building, allowing us to stay focused on the tasks we excel at and become fully transition into that brain required when at work.

Three, we recognize the micro versus the macro. This one takes time, as it's a complete mindset shift. Everyone has their own micro triggers, whether it be the cupboard doors or dishes in the sink, and you should not allow those to impact the bigger picture that you have laid out together. Working through those micro situations allows you to be better prepared together when larger things come into play. What we do is openly communicate—"Hey! You pissed me off today when you . . ."—while we are still in that setting. Once we have left that setting, we let it go. Because dwelling on the small things effects the big things.

Takeaways From Chapter 9

- ❖ Leave your baggage at the door; don't dwell on things you can't control.
- ❖ Be present at home and be present at work; recognize what it takes for your own individual decompression and motivation.
- ❖ Acknowledge, apologize, utilize, work, and learn.

CHAPTER TEN

THE LIFESTYLE ADJUSTMENT

When we first started writing this book, our typical day as a couple running a business looked something like this:

MORNING (PART I):

7:00 a.m.: Fill our coffee mugs with that precious elixir and drive to work. Our thirty-seven-minute commute is when we prime our minds and bodies for the day ahead. This is our time with no distractions, except for the occasional wildlife crossing the road.

7:37–8:00 a.m.: Arrive at work and wrap up coffee time. Because coffee is life, sometimes this lasts a little past eight bells. From here, the work is divided between the front of house (showroom and office) and the back of house (shop, lumber yard).

Robyn—Creates a priority list and checks the schedule for any client appointments.

Clint—Organizes the team's schedule of tasks for the day.

Morning (Part II):

9:00 a.m.: Team arrives. Typically, we have a quick meeting and set off to begin the day's work.

Robyn—Starts at the top of the priority list. These are usually tasks that take the longest and/or have the most benefit for the business.

Clint—Completes a quick email cleanup and makes an inventory of the material needed for the week's projects.

11:00 a.m.: Showroom opens. Meanwhile, the team is busy with builds, installs, and prepping materials in the back.

Noonish: Lunch break (if we have time). Clint usually doesn't stop to eat unless Robyn makes him, although he is coming around to healthier eating habits while working. Years of Gatorade and beef jerky are not kind to the internal organs.

Afternoon:

Back of house: Preparing the next round of installations, and making deliveries and pickups.

4:00 p.m.: Showroom closes.

Robyn—Starts finalizing the details of the day and creates notes for the front of house for tomorrow morning.

5:00 p.m.: Close the shop.

Evening:

6:00 p.m.: Drive home. This is the beginning of decompression time to reflect on the day.

6:37–7:00 p.m.: Dinner prep and chow time.

8:00–9:00 p.m.: Downtime. This usually involves a workout and shower, walking the dog, reading the news, or watching sports.

9:00 p.m.: Bedtime for Robyn. More decompression time for Clint.

10:00 p.m.: Bedtime for Clint.

Repeat.

And that is the pattern of our day-to-day. Was it like that when we first started? Hell, no. Will it be like that in five years? Who knows? But like everything in life and business, we grow, we change, and therefore, we must adapt.

After starting to write this book, we have learned and become more efficient with how we use our time and our space. Our schedules now allow our small business longer manufacturing hours, which is where the bulk of our energy and resources are spent. Robyn is keeping up with the current schedule and working from eight to five. But now, Clint is arriving at the shop at noon and working until 9:00 p.m. There are a few reasons why we made this switch.

Firstly, we pay a lease on a building for twenty-four hours a day. In the past, we were only using it for ten to twelve hours a day, which is about half of the time leased. With the new schedule, we are utilizing our space for twelve to sixteen hours a day.

Secondly, we have outgrown our space and are looking at expansion. However, utilizing the space for more hours is the most cost-effective way to increase production while maintaining costs during a pandemic.

Lastly, the mornings at home are now Clint's time of solitude. They allow him time to complete tasks, such as emails, marketing plans, social media, and outside projects. Put it this way: Clint is not a morning person, but Robyn is. So, this new system allows us to be better as a team mentally and utilize our strengths to the fullest.

Now, when we first met, like a lot of you who may be reading this book, we thought there'd be no chance in hell a schedule like this would work for us. It doesn't. When you're together with someone initially, you're amalgamating two completely separate lives, priorities, and goals, and guess what, there's going to be sacrifices on both ends. One of you may be a firefighter and the other may be a nurse, both on opposite shifts. This makes it tough to find openings in schedules to grow your side hustle if you're planning to start a business together.

Sometimes it's not about making major changes, but rather rethinking the situation you're already in. We could have carried on with the way we always did things, but we discovered room for improvement. We made small changes to make things better. That's the key to innovation and growth. The hardest part is the lifestyle shift because we are all habitual creatures, and let's be honest, change is hard because of the unknown. You don't know if your partner is going to be as engaged as you are in the beginning. You don't know the nonverbal communication cues that can lead to miscommunications. You don't know their strengths and weaknesses and how a change in schedule will affect those.

When it comes to running a business with your spouse, sacrifices have to be made. However, for each decision you make, there has to be a healthy balance for you, your partner, and your business. Each element needs nurturing and attention. Not taking care of your business means it will slowly fade. Not paying attention and working on your relationship means you and your partner might grow apart. But whether you are talking to your spouse about the business or your personal relationship, the basic concepts are the same. You have to talk with your partner and agree on what that balance will be. You may not always agree on what's best, but there has to be a meeting of the minds. It's unfair for one person to make all the sacrifices with the hope that it will all work out for both partners. Hope is nothing without execution. If there is a mutual understanding and a healthy foundation of communication, the possibility of reaching personal and professional goals is well within reach. If you're in the process of deciding to start a business together, take the time to figure out your why. Your why will keep your priorities in alignment and you will always have that motivation because you know why you're doing it.

Takeaways From Chapter 10

- ❖ Learn to develop a cohesive schedule.
- ❖ Always be open to a pivot/change as long as it aligns with the reason that you've decided to get into business with your partner, your reason why.

CHAPTER ELEVEN

BURNOUT

The proverbial hamster wheel is always spinning in our brains. For some of us, it's moving along at a nice walking pace. For others, the hamster is doing more of a jog. And then for people like Clint, there are two hamsters and they are racing in the one-hundred-metre final of the Olympics every single hour he's awake. Robyn attributes Clint's hyperactivity and Type A personality to these duelling hamsters in his brain. Because he wants to focus on about two dozen things at once but has only one pair of eyes and hands, she's often following him around and cleaning up his trail of activity. Some days, Clint will cut a piece of wood for a door or table, then run out for an errand, stop at 7-Eleven for a can of Copenhagen, phone a client, and then three hours later remember there's a piece of wood next to the saw. But this chapter isn't about duelling hamsters. It's about what happens when one of those furry hamster friends falls down and passes out due to exhaustion—or rather, how to prevent that from happening.

The typical day in the shop involves a variety of power tools and machines. Table saws. Mitre saws. Sanders. Drill presses. You name it. To say we've had to repair or replace a few tools over the years is an understatement. They get used over and over and over and then eventually break down. Some survive. Some end up in the cemetery of forgotten tools, never to be seen again.

But just like the tools we use, our bodies and minds have the potential to burn out due to overwork and exhaustion. If we don't charge our batteries each night, and then expect them to work the next day, we would be fools. Similarly, if we don't take time to take care of ourselves, we also run the risk of burning out. And when it happens to a human instead of a piece of machinery, the results are far more impactful on the long-term situation. The experts call it "burnout."

Put simply, burnout can be defined as "a state of emotional, physical and mental exhaustion caused by excessive and prolonged stress . . . [that] cause you to feel helpless, hopeless and resentful."[8] Yikes. It can feel like your brain

---

8 https://www.camh.ca/en/camh-news-and-stories/career-burnout. Accessed Feb. 2021.

is in a dark, heavy cloud, and the things that normally fire with ease just don't. Making decisions and being creative, as well as fostering client and personal relationships, all take an incredible amount of work when you're experiencing burnout. If you've been there—like we have—you know. Although this has probably been happening to humans for centuries, we're here to tell you how we deal with it, but also how we notice it before it kicks our ass. Remember, we are not here to diagnose you, but this is how we notice when its about to hit the fan for us.

Simple Signs You Are Burning Out:

- Slow cognitive function and efficiency
- Poor or impaired decision making
- Anger and resentment over small stuff (e.g., client complaint sets you off, staff issue makes you explode, shortness with your spouse, etc.)
- Brain fog and an uptick in the number of cups of coffee you have in a day
- Unhealthy food choices start becoming more frequent
- Disinterest in hobbies and activities you normally enjoy

- Physical ailments (e.g., back pain, muscle aches, etc.)

But fear not. Hope is not lost. There are many ways to bounce back from burnout and places you can go to for help. We've compiled some tips that should work like a charm because they do for us. And no, it's not a bottle of twenty-one-year-old scotch. Neat.

Firstly, make healthy choices when it comes to food and drinks. Water should be a staple. Whether it's spring, alkaline, or plain old tap water, H2O should be a go-to instead of sugary beverages. When it comes to fuel for the body, there are plenty of options out there. Every once in a while that double cheeseburger and fries can satisfy a craving, but it shouldn't be a regular meal. Foods like that are high in calories and low in substance. They're a quick fix, but not a long-term solution.

Salads and vegetables provide essential nutrients and should make up half of your plate, yet the odd cheese bun and jujube sprinkled in doesn't hurt if you're burning it off. Balance, people. Robyn likes little snacks all day to keep her energy levels up and her focus where it needs to be. During the winter, we pre-make a variety of soups for a couple of reasons. Number one, so Clint eats his lunch. And number two, so Robyn doesn't get hangry at work. In the summer months, we try to make smoothies as often as we can with fresh fruit and produce. But sometimes this doesn't happen, and we end up eating takeout or fast food. We never said we're perfect, and again, it's about balance, not perfection. When your brain hamsters are about to fall off the wheel and pass out, any food to fill the hole will do the trick, just make sure it's actually fuelling your brain and not just a craving because you're tired.

Another easy strategy we use for avoiding burnout is getting enough sleep. If you remember in Chapter 9, we created decompression spaces within our home for ourselves, which allows for adequate recovery. Our bodies need rest, and they function best when all systems are recharged after a solid night of shut-eye. Most adults require about eight hours of sleep, unless you're Robyn and need nine or ten or twelve or thirteen. Being rested is vital for being efficient and staying sharp. How and when you achieve those hours of rest needs to be a part of your conversations with your partner. If you get your best sleep between 5:00 a.m. and 9:00 a.m., you need to figure out a way to work around those hours. If you're a night owl or an early bird, you need to incorporate that into your schedule to be the best version of yourself. This also ties back to previous chapter and learning how to adapt your schedules with your partner as you develop your business and life together.

Being open and honest with your spouse is one of the simplest ways to alleviate stress over time. Tell him or her if you're feeling pissy or grumpy so they have a chance to take cover and brace for impact if things go south. It also allows your partner to take on that meeting or staff issue, so you're not the one dealing with the crying staff member in the office. Or the upset client. Or the difficult supplier. Or whatever else life throws at you. Because sometimes brain fog sets in and it's no joke. The remedy is often to take some time off and escape the phone calls, emails, and the bombardment of demands.

We have a rule that tackles this issue. At least twice a year, we go somewhere remote. No cell service. No Internet access. Three days or even up to a week of escaping everything and everyone but ourselves. These retreats are an oasis for us, but when we were in start-up mode, this wasn't really an option. Now that we are more established, we can get away on these trips and focus on decompression and home mode. This is where having a spouse as a partner is another benefit. We can take vacations at the same time and decompress on the same level. We understand what we're getting away from and what we're going back to. You need to have the right team in place in business to allow for that, or over time, you will burn out.

Burnout can happen if you don't take care of yourself personally. But interpersonally, there is such a huge benefit to having a spouse by your side to lean on and ride the waves with. We recognize that the journey may not always be straight and easy, but when you're on it with your spouse, it's much more enjoyable.

Takeaways From Chapter 11

- ❖ Burnout happens, but it's not the end of the world.
- ❖ There are many ways to avoid burnout before it happens and ways to deal with it when it does.
- ❖ Don't be afraid to take a break and shut off from the company.

CHAPTER TWELVE

WHY WE CONTINUE TO DO IT

All of us have a limited time on this planet. Regardless of where in the world you were born, we all depart at some point. While we're here on Earth, cruising around the sun, we have opportunities each and every day to leave our mark and to grow personally, professionally, intellectually, and emotionally. But that all starts with the right attitude and mindset. There has to be a willingness and desire within. Growth can be painful, but it is also profoundly rewarding. The acorn on the floor of the forest might one day be a mighty oak tree, but it can't do it alone. It needs water, sunlight, shade, and air before it can really develop its roots. All in the right amounts and all at the right time during its development. And just like the oak tree, we need others as we grow, too.

Relationships are complex. They are constantly evolving entities that exist in everything we do. In our personal lives, they exist with our friends and family. In our business lives, we form bonds with our partners, employees, and clients. Each relationship has its own ecosystem and lives and dies based on how we, as individuals, feed it. Even the relationship that we have with a nonliving thing (our business) can be viewed using some of the same criteria. It's important to note the role that sociological and psychological factors, as well as internal and external forces play in our decision-making abilities not only as individuals, but most importantly, as a couple. A brief examination of these four domains will help to answer the question about why we continue to do what we do. It might also give you insight about your own journey and if going into business with your spouse is a good idea or not.

Sociology

Humans are social creatures, so it shouldn't be a surprise that there is an entire field of study related to studying how we engage with each other. This branch of social sciences examines "society, patterns of social relationships, social interaction, and culture that surrounds everyday life."⁹ If a class of university students taking Sociology 101 were studying the day-to-day of our business, they would be in for a treat. We have dynamic relationships on various levels with numerous people. We have to code shift depending on who we're communicating with, which isn't always easy. But it's also part of the reason why we do what we do. The look and the feedback we get from customers after a successful project is hard to put into words. The sense of camaraderie we get from working with each other on a daily basis also forms strong social bonds. Our relationship wouldn't be where it is today if it weren't for the ups and downs we've had with each other. But sociology is just one piece of the puzzle. If sociology is about the external back-and-forth between two or more people, psychology is all about the internal.

Psychology

Psychology is one of those mysterious subjects. What makes us love certain things and despise others? Why are some people drawn toward art and others toward engineering principles? The answer to some of these questions lies within psychology, which involves studying "the way the human mind works and how it influences

---

9   https://www.askdifference.com/anthropology-vs-sociology/. Accessed Feb. 2021.

behaviour."[10] If you really want to do a deep dive into psychology, there are some incredible podcasts out there, and university degrees to be had. For us, the psychology behind why we continue to put our work boots on every single day lies within our passion and commitment to each other and our business. We want to succeed in both our personal and professional aspirations, and we know that the only way we're going to get there is through hard work and dedication. It won't be given. It has to be earned. When we're senior citizens, sipping on our coffees with wrinkled hands and tired eyes, we want to look back on our life and be proud of the time we spent and what we built. Before we get to that stage, though, we not only need to be aware of sociology and psychology, but also internal and external factors that affect us on a daily basis.

Each of us have a unique mental state that affects how we act. Being a married couple in business together means that our relationship is a major investment and is crucial to our success. But that doesn't mean we don't have questions from time to time: Am I strong enough physically, emotionally, and mentally to do this? What happens if we fail? Does my spouse have the "it factor" to push through the difficult times? These are some of the doubts that can consume you if you let them. The mind is a curious thing,

---

10 https://dictionary.cambridge.org/dictionary/english/psychology Accessed Feb. 2021.

and you can utilize it to do incredible things or it can be your downfall. On top of that, there are all of the external factors that come into play.

External And Internal Factors

The external factors are out of our control, but still have an influence on our thought process and behaviour. What we've done together as a couple isn't exactly the norm in the twenty-first century, and we've been faced with an array of challenges that threatened our goals. For Robyn, there has always been the underlying pressure of deciding where to focus most of her time. Family or career? Kids or no kids? The western worldview of family norms is changing, but it still usually involves offspring. And then there's the skyrocketing of divorce rates in our society. We don't want to be another statistic that contributes to that, so as we've mentioned before, we make sure we work on our relationship regularly. In addition to all of those outside factors, there's also investor prejudice against couples and the entrepreneurial mindset problem. However, there is another side of the coin to outside factors that isn't all doom and gloom.

We've built our business like a mosaic. There are bits and pieces of ideas from numerous places, and we've learned a tonne from others. Trade shows, YouTube, parents and grandparents, books—they have all shaped who we are as a company. It's important to learn from others, but not take it as gospel. To have any competitive advantage in our industry, you need to put your own twist on things. Inspiration but not duplication. That's been the same story for generations of creators from musicians to chefs to artists to woodworkers. Techniques are the foundation, but the application of ideas is where the rubber hits the road. And that's what we've tried to do while writing this book.

We firmly believe it's crucial to practise what you preach. So, as we were writing this book, we changed our schedule. We updated our SWOT analysis. We had to apply concepts we were writing about to give credibility to our words. We developed a deeper understanding of ourselves and each other. It forced us to reflect on our journey and try to answer the all-important question: Why do we continue to do it?

Well, some days we have no idea, but we always revert to our why, and other days, we think we have the whole world figured out. But really, when it comes down to it, it's about the love of the game. The dance. The strategy. The process. The execution of an idea. A plan coming to fruition. We both have this internal desire to be better versions of ourselves, and we also both like each other's company more than other people's. Our end goals are the same and we often discuss those at length. We adapt. We change. And we do it together.

As a couple, we have quite literally built hundreds, if not thousands, of projects together, and we continue to build, with purpose, our company and our relationship. It may sound cliché, but it really is about love. This isn't your great-aunt's cheesy romance novel with a shirtless man on the cover, but love really is at the centre of it all. Deep down, both of us share a core belief that we have something truly special together. We are living proof that two people can be successful in their business and personal lives. You too can survive the ins and outs and all the bouts of a business life as a husband and wife.

CONCLUSION

(In Hindsight)

We started writing this book because we wanted to try something new and outside of our regular routine. We thought to ourselves, *What's the worst that can happen?* And then we also asked, What's the best that can happen? Throughout the process of writing this story of how we came to this point in our personal and business lives, we had to really look back and reflect. It made us think back to all the tough times we've had, but also how far we've come. And we couldn't have done it without communication, commitment, and execution. It's one thing to talk about doing something, but it's a whole different game when your actions speak. On this note, we have five core principles to reshare and remind you of the basics of our working relationship and this crazy book idea!

OUR FIVE CORE PRINCIPLES OF COMMUNICATION

- ◈ Trust
- ◈ Honesty
- ◈ Acceptance
- ◈ Balance
- ◈ Sixth sense

We have touched on all these principles throughout this book and truly believe that each one of you can do the same if you so choose to start a business with your spouse. Remember, this book is not gospel, but rather an inside look at what we decided to do as we have journeyed through our relationship and our business.

Effective and seamless communication with your significant other takes time and experience to develop. It won't happen overnight, and it won't always be perfect. Adversity, conflict (both internal and external), success—each of these experiences will hone and sharpen your communication skills if you let them. Dropping the ego and being honest, open, accepting, and a team is the only way. And really, that's why you got married—to find a teammate and go on adventure in this crazy world!

Let's go back: We have given you small tasks and tests to try out with your spouse that will benefit you regardless of whether you're in business together or not. We truly believe in an older school of thought that you work on and fix what's broken and don't have to throw things away. It's why we decided to recycle old barns eight years ago. Everyone has a SWOT analysis to do on themselves to be better, to grow, and to develop a better understanding of yourself and your partner. You also need worldly experience, life experience, and both good and bad experiences, and that's why we think the canoe test is so great! It's a small sample size. It's not the end of the world if shit goes south on a lake unless you can't swim, then make sure you have a life jacket. All joking aside, testing your relationship's boundaries in a microenvironment is a very effective tool, and we think it's healthy because it helps you learn to communicate in a macroenvironment, either verbally or nonverbally.

We have discussed both our viewpoints on separating time from work and home life and given you ideas on how to pivot your lifestyles around not only one another, but also your business goals and life goals. We have shared with you that it's okay to be burnt out and ask for help, and how communicating with your partner in our five ways can make it easier to bounce back and bounce back healthier. We hope you can take something valuable away from this and utilize it in a positive way on your journey.

Lastly, a detail that this process has highlighted for us is that while running a business is a privilege, running a business with your significant other is an incredible gift. We have both learned that growing with one another through the trials and tribulations of entrepreneurship is also a lesson in gratitude and humility. The opportunity to try, whether you succeed or fail, is something that you will never regret. We are living the book. For us, these are not just words on the page; it's life. Thank you for taking the time to read about ours.

To see where we are at now with our business, you can visit www.twobirdsfurniture.ca.

APPENDIX

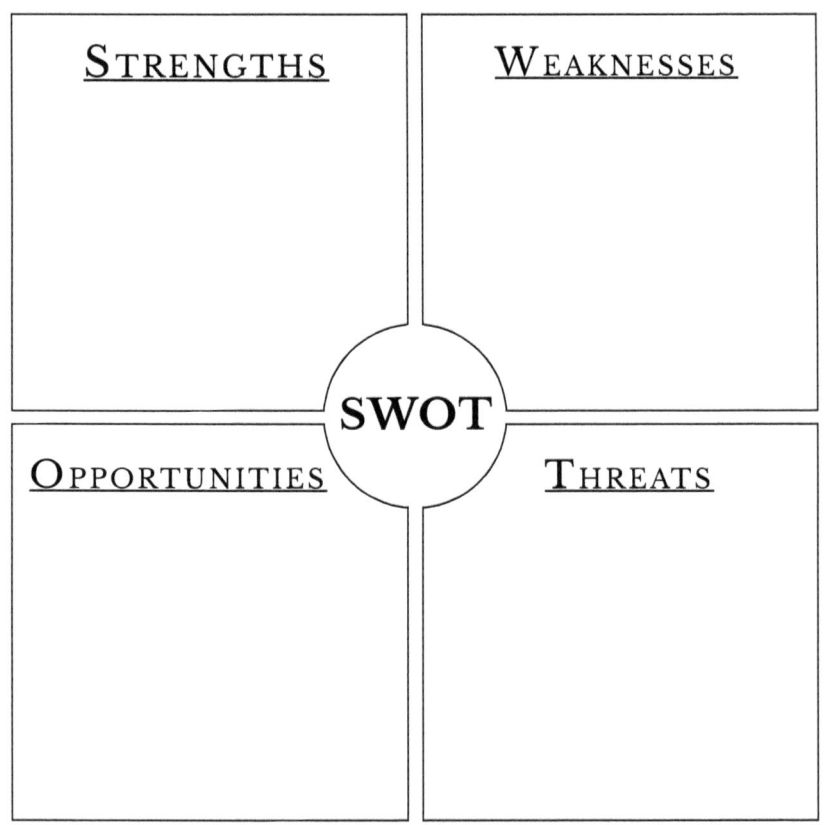

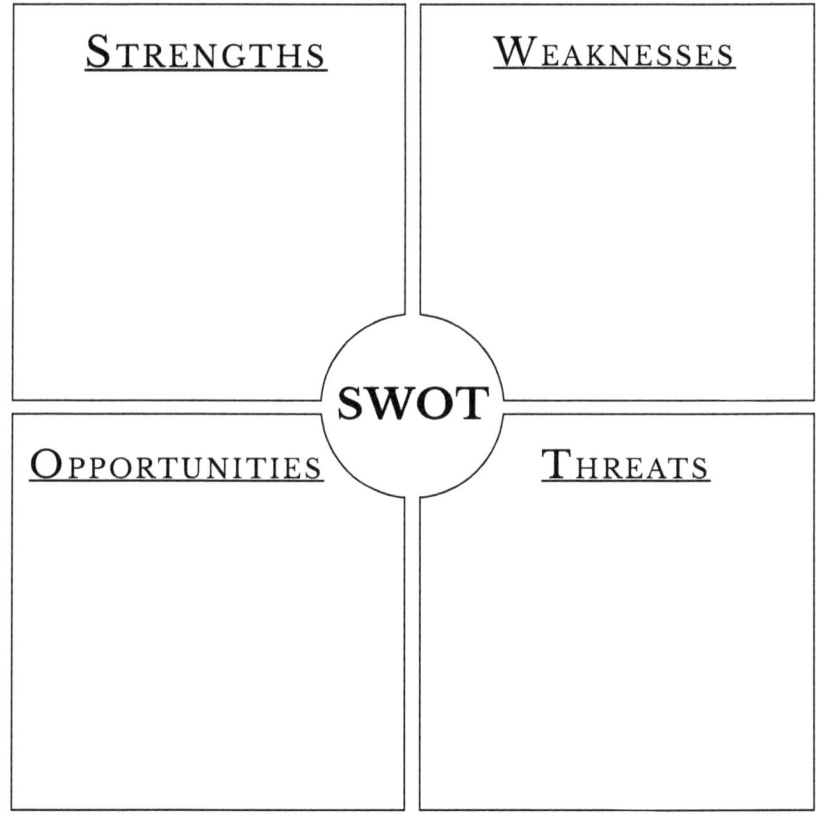

BIBLIOGRAPHY

"Anthropology vs. Sociology." Ask Difference, 17 June 2020, https://www.askdifference.com/anthropology-vs-sociology/. Accessed 12 Feb. 2021.

Aron, A., Norman, C., Aron, E., McKenna, C., & Heyman, R. "Couples' Shared Participation in Novel and Arousing Activities and Experienced Relationship Quality." Journal of Personality And Social Psychology, vol. 78, no. 2, 2000, pp. 273–284. https://doi.org/10.1037/0022-3514.78.2.273.

"Career Burnout." CAMH, 2021, https://www.camh.ca/en/camh-news-and-stories/career-burnout. Accessed 13 Feb. 2021.

DePietro, A. "The Best Business Partner Duos of All Time." Entrepreneur, 1 Aug. 2017, https://www.entrepreneur.com/slideshow/297885#9. Accessed 5 Sept. 2020.

Dreher, B. "This Simple Test Can Predict the Future of Your Relationship." Reader's Digest, 2 Aug. 2019, https://www.rd.com/article/canoe-relationship-test/. Accessed 11 Oct. 2020.

Gasca, Peter. "Understanding Vision and Mission in a Simple Analogy." Inc.com, 28 Jun. 2018, https://www.inc.com/peter-gasca/understanding-vision-mission-in-a-simple-analogy.html. Accessed 29 Aug. 2020.

"Home Data Divorce Rates, By Year of Marriage." Statistics Canada, Table: 39-10-0028-01, 2021, https://www150.statcan.gc.ca/t1/tbl1/en/tv.action?pid=3910002801. Accessed 14 Aug. 2020.

Kenton, W. "Strength, Weakness, Opportunity, and Threat (SWOT) Analysis." Investopedia, 30 Mar. 2020, https://www.investopedia.com/terms/s/swot.asp. Accessed 15 Aug. 2020.

Perez, A. "Why Aristotle Was Right: The Power of Balance." Medium, 6 Mar. 2017, https://medium.com/@perezanthony/why-aristotle-was-right-the-power-of-balance-b743f82edc9f. Accessed 17 Oct. 2020.

"Psychology." Dictionary.cambridge.org, 2021, https://dictionary.cambridge.org/dictionary/english/psychology. Accessed 15 Feb. 2021.

Lightning Source UK Ltd.
Milton Keynes UK
UKHW022240091121
393700UK00011B/438/J